Advanced

Power Query

Techniques

Transforming and Shaping Data
Like a Pro

Kiet Huynh

Table of Contents

CHAPTER I
Introduction to Advanced Power Query Techniques

1.1 Understanding the Power of Power Query

In the realm of data transformation and shaping, Power Query stands as a formidable tool that empowers analysts, data professionals, and enthusiasts to extract, transform, and load data with unprecedented efficiency and flexibility. Its capabilities extend beyond mere data manipulation, allowing users to execute complex transformations and tackle challenging data scenarios effortlessly. In this chapter, we'll delve into the foundational concepts that underpin the power of Power Query and explore its potential through illustrative examples.

Power Query's strength lies in its ability to streamline and automate the data preparation process, irrespective of data source or format. Whether dealing with structured spreadsheets, semi-structured JSON files, or unstructured text, Power Query offers a unified interface for transformation. By visualizing and designing transformations using a user-friendly interface, users can save time and effort that would otherwise be spent writing intricate code.

Benefits of Power Query:

- **Ease of Use:** Power Query's intuitive interface enables users to construct complex transformations through a series of logical steps, making it accessible even to those without programming backgrounds.

- **Data Source Agnostic:** Power Query seamlessly connects to a wide range of data sources, including databases, web services, APIs, and cloud storage solutions, ensuring a consistent transformation approach across diverse data landscapes.

- **Repeatability and Reusability:** Transformations can be recorded and saved as queries, ensuring that the same transformations can be applied to new data with minimal effort. This also enhances collaboration and knowledge sharing within teams.

- Flexibility in Transformation: From basic tasks like filtering and sorting to advanced tasks like merging and aggregating, Power Query provides a versatile toolkit to suit various transformation needs.

- Data Cleansing and Validation: Power Query includes features for handling dirty data, missing values, and outliers, making data cleansing an integral part of the transformation process.

Example:

Let's consider a scenario where you have a dataset containing sales records from multiple regions. You need to aggregate the data to find the total sales for each region, but the dataset is messy with inconsistent naming conventions for regions. Using Power Query, you can standardize region names and perform the aggregation effortlessly.

Step 1: Load the data into Power Query.

Step 2: Create a custom function to map inconsistent region names to standardized ones using a lookup table.

Step 3: Apply the custom function to the region column.

Step 4: Group the data by the standardized region names and calculate the sum of sales for each group.

Step 5: Load the transformed data back into your destination, such as Excel or Power BI.

By following these steps, you not only achieve the desired transformation but also establish a reusable process that can be easily replicated for future data updates.

In conclusion, Power Query is a transformation powerhouse that empowers users to conquer complex data challenges with confidence. This chapter has provided an overview of its potential, and the subsequent chapters will delve into more advanced techniques and strategies that harness the full capabilities of Power Query. Whether you're an analyst, a data scientist, or a business user, mastering these techniques will elevate your data manipulation skills and enhance your ability to extract valuable insights from raw data.

1.2. Navigating Complex Data Transformation Challenges

In the data-driven landscape of today, the ability to efficiently navigate complex data transformation challenges is a skill of paramount importance. This chapter dives into the intricacies of dealing with intricate data transformation scenarios using Advanced Power Query Techniques. We will explore strategies, methodologies, and practical examples to tackle data transformation obstacles that require a sophisticated approach.

Identifying Complex Data Transformation Challenges:

As datasets grow in size and complexity, so do the challenges associated with transforming them. Complex data transformation challenges can include:

1. Data from Multiple Sources: When dealing with data originating from disparate sources, such as databases, spreadsheets, and APIs, harmonizing the data into a unified format can be a formidable task.

2. Irregular Data Structures: Unstructured or semi-structured data, like JSON or XML, often requires intricate parsing and restructuring to extract meaningful insights.

3. Hierarchical Relationships: Data with parent-child or hierarchical relationships, like organizational structures, necessitates specialized techniques to transform and flatten the data effectively.

4. Conditional Transformations: Applying transformations based on conditions can involve intricate logical operations that require a deep understanding of Power Query's capabilities.

5. Time and Date Manipulation: Dealing with time zones, irregular intervals, and extracting specific date components demands advanced skills in date and time transformations.

6. String Manipulation: Textual data might require regular expressions or custom functions to extract, combine, or manipulate information effectively.

Strategies for Complex Data Transformation:

1. Modular Approach: Break down complex transformations into smaller, manageable steps. Transformations can be encapsulated into reusable custom functions, enhancing clarity and maintainability.

2. Parameterization: Utilize parameters to make your transformations dynamic and adaptable to varying scenarios. This enables you to create versatile queries that can be reused across different datasets.

3. Iterative Development: Approach complex transformations iteratively, testing and refining each step before progressing further. This reduces the chances of errors accumulating and simplifies debugging.

4. Error Handling: Implement robust error handling mechanisms to gracefully manage exceptions and irregularities in the data. This prevents transformation failures and ensures the reliability of your query.

Example: Handling Hierarchical Data

Consider a scenario where you have organizational data in a hierarchical format. Each employee has a supervisor, and this nesting continues until the highest-level executive. You need to flatten this hierarchical structure for analysis.

Step 1: Load the hierarchical data into Power Query.

Step 2: Create a custom function that traverses the hierarchy and generates a flattened record for each employee.

Step 3: Apply the custom function to the data, creating a list of flattened records.

Step 4: Expand the list into a table, preserving relevant attributes.

Step 5: Load the flattened data for further analysis.

By approaching this challenge systematically and leveraging custom functions, you can successfully transform complex hierarchical data into a more accessible format.

In conclusion, this chapter has introduced the complexities of navigating intricate data transformation challenges. By recognizing the diverse scenarios that demand advanced Power Query techniques, you're better prepared to tackle these challenges head-on. As we progress through this book, we will delve deeper into specific techniques, strategies, and case studies that showcase the power of Power Query in overcoming complex data transformation hurdles.

CHAPTER II
Advanced Data Loading Strategies

2.1 Parallel Loading for Enhanced Performance

Efficient data loading is crucial for managing large datasets and ensuring timely analysis. In this chapter, we will delve into advanced data loading strategies, starting with the concept of parallel loading. Parallel loading is a technique that exploits the power of modern hardware to load data from multiple sources simultaneously, significantly boosting loading speed and overall performance. We'll explore the benefits, considerations, and practical implementation of parallel loading using Power Query.

Benefits of Parallel Loading:

Parallel loading offers several advantages, especially when dealing with massive datasets:

1. Faster Data Loading: Loading data in parallel from multiple sources can dramatically reduce loading times, utilizing the capabilities of modern multi-core processors.

2. Optimal Resource Utilization: By distributing the loading process across multiple cores, you ensure that your hardware resources are used more efficiently.

3. Scalability: As your datasets grow, parallel loading remains a scalable solution, maintaining loading speed even with increased data volumes.

Considerations for Parallel Loading:

While parallel loading can yield impressive results, a few considerations need to be addressed:

1. Data Source Compatibility: Not all data sources are compatible with parallel loading. Ensure that the sources you are using can be queried in parallel.

2. Data Transformation: Complex transformations applied during loading might impact the effectiveness of parallel loading. Evaluate whether these transformations can be applied after the data is loaded.

3. Resource Availability: Parallel loading consumes more system resources, so ensure your hardware can handle the increased workload without performance degradation.

Implementing Parallel Loading:

Let's consider an example where you have to load data from multiple CSV files into a single dataset. Each CSV file contains information about different product categories, and you want to combine them into one consolidated table.

Step 1: Load CSV Files in Parallel

- Create a list of file paths for all CSV files using the `Folder.Files` function.

- Use the `Table.AddColumn` function to add a custom column that loads each CSV file using `Csv.Document`.

Step 2: Combine Loaded Data

- Create a new query that appends all loaded data together using the `Table.Combine` function.

Step 3: Apply Additional Transformations

- Perform any necessary transformations on the combined dataset, such as data type conversions or filtering.

Step 4: Load the Final Transformed Data

- Load the final transformed dataset into your destination, such as Power BI or Excel.

Example:

Let's say you have 10 CSV files, each containing sales data for different product categories. By loading these CSV files in parallel and combining the results, you can significantly reduce loading time.

Conclusion:

Parallel loading is a powerful technique for optimizing data loading performance, especially when dealing with large and diverse datasets. By understanding its benefits, considerations, and implementation steps, you can harness the capabilities of modern hardware to speed up your data loading processes. As you advance in your Power Query journey, incorporating parallel loading into your workflow will enhance your ability to handle big data efficiently and drive insights faster.

2.2. Incremental Loading: Extracting Only What's Needed

Efficient data loading is not just about speed; it's also about minimizing resource consumption and ensuring data remains up-to-date. In this chapter, we'll explore the concept of incremental loading, a powerful strategy that involves extracting only new or modified data from the source since the last load. Incremental loading not only saves time and resources but also helps maintain data integrity. We'll delve into the benefits, considerations, and step-by-step implementation of incremental loading using Power Query.

Benefits of Incremental Loading:

Incremental loading offers several advantages for data processing workflows:

1. Faster Loading: By loading only the changed or new data, incremental loading reduces the overall loading time compared to full data loads.

2. Reduced Resource Consumption: Incremental loading minimizes the impact on system resources, as you're dealing with smaller datasets.

3. Data Integrity: Loading only the delta (changes) preserves data integrity and consistency.

Considerations for Incremental Loading:

While incremental loading is efficient, several factors need consideration:

1. Source Compatibility: Not all data sources support efficient tracking of changes. Databases that maintain change logs or timestamps are more suitable for incremental loading.

2. Timestamp or Identifier: You need a reliable timestamp or unique identifier in your data to track changes accurately.

3. Data Growth: Incremental loading is particularly useful when data grows over time. If your data seldom changes, full loading might be more efficient.

Implementing Incremental Loading:

Let's take a practical example where you're loading sales data from a database and want to implement incremental loading.

Step 1: Initial Full Load

- Load the entire dataset from the source using Power Query.

Step 2: Capture Last Load Timestamp

- After the initial load, record the timestamp of the load completion.

Step 3: Retrieve Changes Since Last Load

- On subsequent loads, query the source for data with timestamps greater than the recorded timestamp.

Step 4: Combine New Data

- Combine the new data with the existing dataset.

Step 5: Apply Transformations

- Apply any necessary transformations to the combined dataset.

Step 6: Load the Final Transformed Data

- Load the final transformed dataset into your destination.

Example:

Assume you're working with a sales database that has a "LastModified" timestamp column. You initially load all sales data into Power Query. For incremental loads, you query the database for data with a "LastModified" timestamp greater than the recorded timestamp from the last load.

Conclusion:

Incremental loading is a vital strategy for maintaining data currency and efficiency. By understanding its benefits and following the step-by-step implementation approach, you can ensure that your data processing workflows are not only faster but also consume fewer resources. Incremental loading is particularly valuable for scenarios where data changes over time, allowing you to stay up-to-date while minimizing the impact on your infrastructure. As you progress in your data transformation journey, incorporating incremental loading into your toolkit will enhance your ability to manage and utilize data effectively.

2.3. API Integration and Web Data Retrieval

In today's data-driven landscape, the availability of external data sources through APIs has opened up new avenues for insights. This chapter delves into the intricacies of API integration and web data retrieval using Power Query. We will explore how to harness the power of APIs to seamlessly retrieve data from online sources, perform transformations, and integrate it into your data workflows. Through practical examples and step-by-step guidance, you'll learn to tap into the wealth of information available on the web.

Benefits of API Integration and Web Data Retrieval:

API integration and web data retrieval offer several benefits:

1. Access to Fresh Data: APIs provide real-time or near-real-time data updates, ensuring your analysis is based on the latest information.

2. Diverse Data Sources: APIs give you access to a vast range of data sources, from social media platforms to financial data providers.

3. Automation: Once configured, API-based data retrieval can be automated to regularly fetch and update your data, reducing manual efforts.

Considerations for API Integration:

API integration involves a few key considerations:

1. API Documentation: Understand the API's documentation, endpoints, request parameters, and authentication methods.

2. Rate Limits: Many APIs impose rate limits to prevent abuse. Ensure your integration respects these limits.

3. Data Format: APIs typically return data in JSON or XML format. You'll need to parse and transform this data into a usable format.

Implementing API Integration and Web Data Retrieval:

Let's consider a scenario where you want to retrieve real-time weather data from a weather API and integrate it into your dataset.

Step 1: API Registration and Authentication

- Register for an API key on the weather service provider's website.

- Use the API key to authenticate your requests to the API.

Step 2: Build API Request URL

- Identify the API's endpoint and any required parameters.

- Construct the API request URL, including the API key and any necessary parameters.

Step 3: Retrieve Data Using Power Query

- In Power Query, use the `Web.Contents` function to make an HTTP GET request to the API URL.

- Parse the JSON response using the `Json.Document` function to convert it into a usable format.

Step 4: Transform and Integrate Data

- Apply necessary transformations to the retrieved data, such as filtering, renaming columns, or converting data types.

Step 5: Combine with Existing Data

- If needed, merge the retrieved data with your existing dataset.

Step 6: Load the Final Transformed Data

- Load the combined and transformed data into your destination.

Example:

Suppose you're working on a retail analysis project and want to include weather data for different regions. You can integrate weather data using an API like OpenWeatherMap, which provides weather information based on location.

Conclusion:

API integration and web data retrieval have become essential skills for data professionals seeking diverse and up-to-date sources of information. By understanding the principles of API authentication, constructing request URLs, and parsing JSON responses, you can seamlessly integrate web data into your analysis workflows. As you navigate the vast landscape of APIs, you'll find opportunities to enhance your analyses, gain insights from real-time data, and automate your data retrieval processes. This chapter has provided an essential foundation for leveraging APIs in your data transformation journey.

CHAPTER III
Data Transformation Beyond Basics

3.1 Unpivoting and Pivoting Complex Data Structures

Data rarely comes in the exact format you need for analysis. It often requires restructuring to make it more conducive to insights. This chapter explores advanced data transformation techniques: unpivoting and pivoting, using Power Query. We'll uncover how to reshape complex data structures to extract valuable information. Through concrete examples and step-by-step instructions, you'll gain mastery over these pivotal transformations.

Unpivoting Data:

Unpivoting involves converting columns into rows, ideal for transforming data with multiple measures into a more analyzable format.

Example:

Suppose you have a dataset with columns representing sales by quarter (Q1, Q2, Q3, Q4) for different products. To perform meaningful analysis, you need to unpivot the data into two columns: "Product" and "Quarterly Sales."

Step 1: Load Data

- Load the dataset into Power Query.

Step 2: Unpivot Columns

- Select the columns containing the quarter-wise sales data.

- Use the "Unpivot Columns" option under the "Transform" tab to convert the columns into rows.

- Rename the new columns as "Product" and "Quarterly Sales."

Step 3: Load Transformed Data

- Load the unpivoted data into your destination for analysis.

Pivoting Data:

Pivoting involves converting unique values from a column into new columns, condensing data and enabling easier analysis.

Example:

Imagine you have sales data with products and quarterly sales figures, but you want to pivot it to show each product's sales across different quarters.

Step 1: Load Data

- Load the dataset into Power Query.

Step 2: Pivot Data

- Select the column containing the quarter information.

- Use the "Pivot Column" option under the "Transform" tab.

- Choose the "Values Column" as the one containing sales figures.

- Rename the new columns with the quarter names.

Step 3: Load Transformed Data

- Load the pivoted data for analysis.

Combining Unpivoting and Pivoting:

Sometimes, you might need to perform both unpivoting and pivoting in a sequence to transform your data optimally.

Example:

Consider a dataset with regional sales figures, where each region's sales are presented quarterly. To analyze trends, you want to pivot the quarters into rows, but within each region.

Step 1: Load Data

- Load the dataset into Power Query.

Step 2: Unpivot Columns for Quarters

- Unpivot the columns representing quarterly sales for all regions except the region column.

Step 3: Pivot Quarter Data by Region

- Pivot the column with quarter names.

- Choose the "Values Column" as the one containing the quarterly sales figures.

- Rename the new columns according to quarters.

Step 4: Load Transformed Data

- Load the data into your destination for analysis.

Conclusion:

Unpivoting and pivoting are potent data transformation techniques that empower you to reshape complex data structures for effective analysis. By mastering these techniques and applying them to various scenarios, you can unlock valuable insights from your data. Whether you're working with sales data, survey responses, or any other dataset with multidimensional attributes, the ability to adeptly unpivot and pivot will significantly enhance your data manipulation prowess. This chapter has laid the foundation for your journey into advanced data transformations, equipping you with the tools to conquer even the most intricate datasets.

3.2. Handling Hierarchical Data: Parent-Child Relationships

In the realm of data transformation, hierarchical data structures pose unique challenges. This chapter delves into advanced techniques for handling parent-child relationships within datasets using Power Query. We'll explore strategies for transforming hierarchical data into a more analyzable format, unraveling the complexities through real-world examples and comprehensive guidance.

Understanding Parent-Child Relationships:

Hierarchical data represents relationships between entities, often involving parent-child connections. Examples include organizational structures, family trees, or product categories with subcategories. Transforming such data into a tabular format facilitates easier analysis.

Example:

Imagine you have a dataset representing an organizational structure, where each employee has a supervisor identified by their ID. You want to flatten this hierarchy to analyze performance across all employees.

Step 1: Load Hierarchical Data

- Load the hierarchical data into Power Query.

Step 2: Create a Recursive Function

- Write a custom function that takes an employee ID and retrieves their supervisor's information.

- This function will call itself recursively until it reaches the top-level supervisor.

Step 3: Apply Recursive Function

- Use the custom function to create a new column containing the supervisor's information for each employee.

Step 4: Load Transformed Data

- Load the flattened data into your destination for analysis.

Flattening Hierarchical Data:

Flattening hierarchical data involves transforming nested structures into a tabular format.

Example:

Suppose you have a dataset containing product categories and subcategories in a hierarchical format. You want to flatten this structure for easier analysis.

Step 1: Load Hierarchical Data

- Load the hierarchical data into Power Query.

Step 2: Expand Subcategories

- Use the "Expand" option under the "Transform" tab to expand the subcategories column.

- This will duplicate rows for each subcategory, maintaining the relevant parent information.

Step 3: Load Transformed Data

- Load the flattened data into your destination for analysis.

Creating Hierarchical Aggregations:

Analyzing hierarchical data often involves aggregating values at different levels of the hierarchy.

Example:

Consider the previous organizational structure dataset. You want to calculate the total sales for each supervisor, aggregating the sales of their subordinates.

Step 1: Load Hierarchical Data

- Load the hierarchical data into Power Query.

Step 2: Calculate Aggregations

- Create a new column that calculates each employee's sales.

- Use Power Query's "Group By" feature to aggregate sales for each supervisor, summing the sales of their subordinates.

Step 3: Load Aggregated Data

- Load the aggregated data into your destination for analysis.

Conclusion:

Handling parent-child relationships in hierarchical data structures is an advanced data transformation skill that enhances your analytical capabilities. By adeptly navigating hierarchical relationships, you can uncover insights hidden within complex datasets. Whether you're dealing with organizational charts, genealogical data, or any other hierarchical dataset, the ability to transform and analyze such data efficiently is a valuable asset. This chapter has provided you with the tools to master hierarchical data transformation, empowering you to unravel intricate relationships and glean actionable insights from even the most intricate datasets.

3.3. Working with Multi-Dimensional Data

In the world of data transformation, multi-dimensional data adds a layer of complexity. This chapter delves into advanced techniques for handling multi-dimensional data using Power Query. We'll explore strategies for transforming and analyzing multi-dimensional data, providing tangible examples and step-by-step guidance to navigate through these intricate scenarios.

Understanding Multi-Dimensional Data:

Multi-dimensional data involves data with more than two dimensions, such as data cubes. It's common in scenarios like sales analysis with dimensions like time, product, and location. Transforming and analyzing this data necessitates special techniques.

Example:

Imagine you have a dataset representing sales across different products, time periods, and regions. Each combination forms a unique intersection with corresponding sales values. You want to transform this multi-dimensional data into a tabular format for analysis.

Step 1: Load Multi-Dimensional Data

- Load the multi-dimensional data into Power Query.

Step 2: Unpivot Data

- Unpivot the data, converting the multi-dimensional matrix into a tabular format.

- You'll end up with columns for dimensions (product, time, region) and a column for the corresponding sales values.

Step 3: Load Transformed Data

- Load the unpivoted data into your destination for analysis.

Creating Multi-Dimensional Aggregations:

Analyzing multi-dimensional data involves aggregating values across multiple dimensions.

Example:

Consider the previous sales dataset. You want to calculate the total sales for each product across different time periods and regions.

Step 1: Load Multi-Dimensional Data

- Load the multi-dimensional data into Power Query.

Step 2: Group and Aggregate

- Use Power Query's "Group By" feature to aggregate sales values based on dimensions like product, time, and region.

Step 3: Load Aggregated Data

- Load the aggregated data into your destination for analysis.

Visualizing Multi-Dimensional Data:

Visualization is crucial for understanding multi-dimensional data. Using pivot tables or charts can help you grasp complex relationships.

Example:

Taking the previous sales dataset, you want to visualize total sales across products, time periods, and regions using a pivot table.

Step 1: Load Multi-Dimensional Data

- Load the multi-dimensional data into Power Query.

Step 2: Pivot Data

- Use Power Query's "Pivot Column" feature to pivot the data based on dimensions.

- Choose the "Values Column" as the sales values.

Step 3: Create Pivot Table

- Load the pivoted data into Excel.

- Create a pivot table and arrange dimensions in rows and columns.

- Place sales values in the value area.

Step 4: Visualize Data

- The pivot table provides an interactive view of multi-dimensional data, helping you analyze patterns.

Conclusion:

Working with multi-dimensional data requires advanced techniques to transform, analyze, and visualize complex relationships. By mastering these techniques, you can unravel insights from intricate datasets with multiple dimensions. Whether you're analyzing sales, customer behavior, or any other multi-dimensional dataset, the ability to navigate this complexity is a valuable asset. This chapter has equipped you with the skills to confidently manipulate and analyze multi-dimensional data, empowering you to uncover actionable insights even in the most intricate   datasets.

CHAPTER IV
Advanced Text and String Manipulation

4.1 Regular Expressions for Advanced Text Extraction

In the realm of data manipulation, text processing plays a pivotal role in extracting valuable insights from unstructured data. This chapter dives into advanced text and string manipulation techniques using Power Query, with a focus on employing regular expressions. Through concrete examples and step-by-step guidance, you'll learn how to harness the power of regular expressions to extract specific patterns from text data.

Understanding Regular Expressions:

Regular expressions (regex) are powerful patterns that define text search and manipulation rules. They are a versatile tool for identifying complex patterns in text and extracting desired information.

Example:

Suppose you have a dataset containing email addresses, and you want to extract the domain names (e.g., "example.com") from each email.

Step 1: Load Text Data

- Load the dataset containing email addresses into Power Query.

Step 2: Apply Regular Expression

- Use the `Text.RegexReplace` function to apply a regular expression pattern that captures the domain name.

- The pattern might be: `@"@(.+)$"` which captures the domain after the "@" symbol.

Step 3: Extracted Domain Data

- Load the extracted domain data into your destination for analysis.

Advanced Text Extraction:

Regular expressions offer sophisticated ways to extract complex information from text.

Example:

Imagine you have a dataset containing product codes in the format "AB12345," where "AB" is the category code and "12345" is the product number. You want to extract both components.

Step 1: Load Text Data

- Load the dataset containing product codes into Power Query.

Step 2: Apply Regular Expression

- Use the `Text.RegexMatch` function to apply a regular expression pattern to capture the category and product number.

- The pattern might be: `@"([A-Z]{2})(\d{5})"` which captures two uppercase letters (category) followed by five digits (product number).

Step 3: Extracted Components

- Load the extracted category and product number data into your destination for analysis.

Replacing Text with Regular Expressions:

Regular expressions can also be used to replace specific patterns within text.

Example:

Consider a dataset containing free-form addresses, and you want to standardize them by removing unnecessary punctuation.

Step 1: Load Text Data

- Load the dataset containing addresses into Power Query.

Step 2: Apply Regular Expression Replacement

- Use the `Text.RegexReplace` function with a pattern that matches unwanted punctuation.

- Replace the matched pattern with an empty string to remove it.

Step 3: Standardized Addresses

- Load the standardized address data into your destination for analysis.

Conclusion:

Regular expressions are a potent tool for advanced text and string manipulation in data transformation. By understanding and harnessing their capabilities, you can efficiently extract specific patterns from unstructured text data. Whether you're cleaning, extracting, or transforming text, regular expressions offer a versatile approach to handling complex patterns. This chapter has provided you with the foundation to confidently wield regular expressions, enabling you to extract valuable insights from text data and streamline your data transformation workflows.

4.2. Combining Multiple Text Columns Strategically

Data often resides across multiple columns, and combining text from these columns can provide valuable insights. This chapter explores advanced techniques for combining and manipulating text from multiple columns using Power Query. Through practical examples and step-by-step guidance, you'll learn how to strategically merge and transform text to enhance your data transformation toolkit.

Combining Text Columns:

Strategically combining text from multiple columns is essential for creating informative labels, identifiers, or composite data points.

Example:

Imagine you have a dataset containing first names and last names of customers, and you want to create a column that combines both names for use as a salutation.

Step 1: Load Text Data

- Load the dataset containing first names and last names into Power Query.

Step 2: Combine Text Columns

- Use the `Table.AddColumn` function to create a new column that concatenates the first name, a space, and the last name.

- For example: `Table.AddColumn(Source, "Salutation", each [First Name] & " " & [Last Name])`.

Step 3: Load Combined Data

- Load the dataset with the new salutation column into your destination.

Advanced Text Manipulation:

Combining text can involve more complex transformations.

Example:

Suppose you have a dataset containing product names, categories, and prices, and you want to create a column that generates an abbreviated product code.

Step 1: Load Text Data

- Load the dataset containing product names, categories, and prices into Power Query.

Step 2: Create Abbreviated Code

- Use the `Table.AddColumn` function to create a new column that takes the first two characters of the category, followed by the first two characters of the product name, and the last two digits of the price.

- For example: `Table.AddColumn(Source, "Product Code", each Text.Start([Category], 2) & Text.Start([Product Name], 2) & Text.End(Text.From([Price]), 2))`.

Step 3: Load Abbreviated Codes

- Load the dataset with the new product code column into your destination.

Conditional Text Manipulation:

Conditional logic can determine how text from multiple columns is combined.

Example:

Consider a dataset containing sales records with product names, quantities, and discount levels. You want to create a column that includes a discount indication only for products with discounts.

Step 1: Load Text Data

- Load the dataset containing product names, quantities, and discount levels into Power Query.

Step 2: Create Conditional Text

- Use the `Table.AddColumn` function to create a new column that checks if the discount level is greater than zero.

- If true, concatenate " (Discount Available)" to the product name; otherwise, keep the product name as is.

- For example: `Table.AddColumn(Source, "Product Name with Discount", each [Product Name] & If([Discount] > 0, " (Discount Available)", ""))`.

Step 3: Load Conditional Text Data

- Load the dataset with the new product name column into your destination.

Conclusion:

Strategically combining text from multiple columns is an advanced skill that enriches your data transformation capabilities. By understanding these techniques and their applications, you can create informative, composite data points that enhance the insights derived from your data. Whether you're building salutations, codes, or custom labels, the ability to skillfully manipulate and combine text is a valuable asset. This chapter has equipped you with the tools to confidently manipulate and enhance text data, allowing you to craft richer narratives and insights from your transformed data.

4.3. Custom Functions for Complex String Operations

Complex string operations often require custom solutions that go beyond built-in functions. This chapter delves into the creation and utilization of custom functions for intricate text manipulation tasks using Power Query. Through detailed examples and step-by-step instructions, you'll learn how to design and implement custom functions to tackle the most challenging text-related transformations.

Creating Custom Functions:

Custom functions empower you to encapsulate complex logic and reuse it across your transformation workflows.

Example:

Consider a dataset with product descriptions containing various symbols and non-alphanumeric characters. You want to create a custom function that removes all non-alphanumeric characters to clean up the descriptions.

Step 1: Load Text Data

- Load the dataset containing product descriptions into Power Query.

Step 2: Design Custom Function

- Under the "View" tab, select "Advanced Editor" to access Power Query's scripting interface.

- Write a custom function using M-language that accepts a text input and removes non-alphanumeric characters using `Text.Select`.

```M
let
    RemoveNonAlphanumeric = (text) =>
        Text.Select(text, {"0".."9", "a".."z", "A".."Z"}),
    Source = YourSource,
    CleanedDescriptions = Table.AddColumn(Source, "Cleaned Description", each RemoveNonAlphanumeric([Description]))
in
    CleanedDescriptions
```

Step 3: Load Data with Custom Function

- Load the dataset with the newly created column into your destination.

Handling Dynamic Text Manipulation:

Custom functions can also adapt to different scenarios by accepting parameters.

Example:

Suppose you have a dataset with product names, and you want to create custom abbreviations based on user-defined maximum lengths.

Step 1: Load Text Data

- Load the dataset containing product names into Power Query.

Step 2: Design Parameterized Custom Function

- Create a custom function that accepts a text input and a maximum length parameter.

- If the text length is greater than the parameter, truncate it and append ellipsis ("...").

```M
let
    AbbreviateText = (text, maxLength) =>
        if Text.Length(text) > maxLength then
            Text.Start(text, maxLength - 3) & "..."
        else
            text,
    Source = YourSource,
    AbbreviatedProducts = Table.AddColumn(Source, "Abbreviated Name", each
AbbreviateText([Product Name], 10))
in
    AbbreviatedProducts
```

Step 3: Load Data with Parameterized Custom Function

- Load the dataset with the newly created column into your destination.

Utilizing Recursive Custom Functions:

Recursive custom functions enable intricate string manipulations that require iteration.

Example:

Consider a dataset with nested strings, and you want to create a custom function that extracts the innermost text within parentheses.

Step 1: Load Text Data

- Load the dataset containing nested strings into Power Query.

Step 2: Design Recursive Custom Function

- Create a custom function that recursively extracts text between parentheses.

- The function keeps searching for innermost text within parentheses until there's no more nesting.

```M
let
    ExtractInnermost = (text) =>
        if Text.PositionOf(text, "(") <> -1 then
            let
                start = Text.PositionOf(text, "(") + 1,
                end = Text.PositionOf(text, ")")
            in
                ExtractInnermost(Text.Middle(text, start, end - start))
        else
            text,
    Source = YourSource,
    ExtractedText     =     Table.AddColumn(Source,     "Extracted     Text",     each
ExtractInnermost([Nested String]))
```

in

    ExtractedText

```

**Step 3:** Load Data with Recursive Custom Function

- Load the dataset with the newly created column into your destination.

**Conclusion:**

Creating custom functions for complex string operations is an advanced skill that empowers you to handle intricate text manipulations effectively. By crafting these functions, you can efficiently address unique text-related challenges and integrate them seamlessly into your transformation workflows. Whether you're cleaning, abbreviating, or extracting text, custom functions offer a versatile and reusable approach. This chapter has provided you with the foundation to confidently design and implement custom functions, elevating your text manipulation capabilities and enabling you to tackle the most demanding data transformation tasks.
```

CHAPTER V
Conditional Logic and Error Handling

5.1 Advanced Conditional Transformations

Conditional logic is the backbone of data transformation, allowing you to apply rules based on specific conditions. This chapter delves into advanced conditional transformations using Power Query, demonstrating how to implement intricate logic to manipulate and structure your data. Through detailed examples and step-by-step instructions, you'll learn how to leverage conditional statements to achieve sophisticated data transformations.

Using Conditional Transformations:

Advanced conditional transformations involve applying complex rules to data based on conditions.

Example:

Suppose you have a dataset containing sales data with product names and quantities, and you want to classify products as "High," "Medium," or "Low" based on their sales quantities.

Step 1: Load Data

- Load the dataset containing product names and quantities into Power Query.

Step 2: Implement Conditional Logic

- Use the `Table.AddColumn` function to create a new column that assigns a classification based on sales quantities.

- Utilize nested `if` statements or the `if-then-else` function for multi-condition logic.

```M
let
    ClassifyProduct = (quantity) =>
        if quantity > 100 then "High"
        else if quantity > 50 then "Medium"
        else "Low",
    Source = YourSource,
    ClassifiedProducts        =      Table.AddColumn(Source,      "Classification",        each
ClassifyProduct([Quantity]))
in
    ClassifiedProducts
```

Step 3: Load Data with Classification

- Load the dataset with the new classification column into your destination.

Conditional Column Creation:

Advanced conditional transformations can lead to creating entirely new columns based on conditions.

Example:

Imagine you have a dataset with order dates, and you want to create a column indicating whether an order was made during a holiday season.

Step 1: Load Data

- Load the dataset containing order dates into Power Query.

Step 2: Create Conditional Column

- Use the `Table.AddColumn` function to create a new column that checks if an order date falls within a predefined holiday season.

- This can be achieved using the `if-then-else` function or the `if` statement.

```M
let
    IsHolidaySeason = (date) =>
        if Date.Month(date) = 12 then "Holiday Season"
        else if Date.Month(date) = 11 then "Pre-Holiday Season"
        else "Regular Season",
    Source = YourSource,
    OrderDataWithSeason = Table.AddColumn(Source, "Season", each IsHolidaySeason([Order Date]))
in
    OrderDataWithSeason
```

Step 3: Load Data with Conditional Column

- Load the dataset with the new season column into your destination.

Applying Complex Conditions:

Advanced conditional transformations may involve combining multiple conditions.

Example:

Suppose you have a dataset with customer data, and you want to classify customers based on their purchase history and age.

Step 1: Load Data

- Load the dataset containing customer data into Power Query.

Step 2: Implement Complex Conditional Logic

- Use the `Table.AddColumn` function to create a new column that combines multiple conditions for customer classification.

- You can use logical operators (`and`, `or`) and nested `if` statements.

```M
let
    ClassifyCustomer = (age, totalPurchases) =>
        if age > 50 and totalPurchases > 1000 then "High Value"
        else if age > 30 and totalPurchases > 500 then "Medium Value"
        else "Low Value",
    Source = YourSource,
    ClassifiedCustomers = Table.AddColumn(Source, "Customer Value", each ClassifyCustomer([Age], [Total Purchases]))
in
```

ClassifiedCustomers

```
```

Step 3: Load Data with Customer Classification

- Load the dataset with the new customer value column into your destination.

Conclusion:

Advanced conditional transformations are essential for tailoring data to specific conditions, enabling you to create nuanced insights from your datasets. By mastering these techniques and applying them to your data, you can unlock complex transformations that enhance your analytical capabilities. Whether you're classifying, segmenting, or flagging data, the ability to adeptly use conditional logic is a valuable asset. This chapter has equipped you with the skills to confidently implement advanced conditional transformations, allowing you to perform intricate data manipulations that drive deeper insights and understanding.

5.2. Handling Errors and Irregular Data

In the realm of data transformation, handling errors and irregularities is crucial for maintaining data integrity and ensuring accurate analysis. This chapter explores advanced techniques for managing errors and addressing irregular data scenarios using Power Query. Through practical examples and step-by-step guidance, you'll learn how to implement robust error handling mechanisms and strategies to deal with data inconsistencies effectively.

Error Handling Strategies:

Advanced error handling involves detecting, addressing, and even preventing errors that can arise during data transformation.

Example:

Suppose you have a dataset containing sales records, but some rows have missing or invalid values in the "Quantity" column. You want to replace these errors with a default value.

Step 1: Load Data

- Load the dataset containing sales records into Power Query.

Step 2: Implement Error Handling

- Use the `Table.AddColumn` function to create a new column that checks for errors in the "Quantity" column.

- If an error is detected (e.g., null or non-numeric value), replace it with a default value.

```M
let
    HandleQuantityErrors = (quantity) =>
        if Value.Is(value, type number) then value else 0,
    Source = YourSource,
    HandledData    =    Table.AddColumn(Source,    "Handled    Quantity",    each
HandleQuantityErrors([Quantity]))
in
    HandledData
```

Step 3: Load Data with Error Handling

- Load the dataset with the new column that handles quantity errors into your destination.

Dealing with Missing Values:

Handling missing values requires specialized techniques to ensure your analysis isn't compromised.

Example:

Consider a dataset containing customer information, but some rows have missing values in the "Email" column. You want to replace these missing values with a placeholder.

Step 1: Load Data

- Load the dataset containing customer information into Power Query.

Step 2: Replace Missing Values

- Use the `Table.ReplaceValue` function to replace all occurrences of the missing value (e.g., null) with a placeholder value.

```M
let
    ReplaceMissingEmail = (email) =>
        if email = null then "[No Email]" else email,
    Source = YourSource,
    ReplacedEmails = Table.ReplaceValue(Source, null, "[No Email]", Replacer.ReplaceValue, {"Email"})
in
    ReplacedEmails
```

Step 3: Load Data with Replaced Values

- Load the dataset with the "Email" column containing replaced missing values into your destination.

Handling Inconsistent Formats:

Data inconsistency, such as varying date formats, requires standardization for accurate analysis.

Example:

Suppose you have a dataset with date columns, but some dates are in different formats. You want to standardize them to a consistent format.

Step 1: Load Data

- Load the dataset containing date columns into Power Query.

Step 2: Standardize Date Formats

- Use the `Date.ToText` function to convert date values to a consistent format.

- Apply the function to all date columns.

```M
let
    Source = YourSource,
    StandardizedDates = Table.TransformColumns(Source, {"Date Column", each Date.ToText(_, "yyyy-MM-dd")})
```

in

StandardizedDates

```

**Step 3:** Load Data with Standardized Dates

- Load the dataset with date columns containing standardized formats into your destination.

**Conclusion:**

Handling errors and irregular data is an advanced skill that ensures the accuracy and reliability of your data transformation workflows. By mastering these techniques, you can mitigate risks associated with inconsistent or erroneous data. Whether you're addressing missing values, standardizing formats, or preventing errors, effective error handling is a cornerstone of data quality and integrity. This chapter has provided you with the tools to confidently implement advanced error handling and data consistency strategies, allowing you to maintain the reliability of your transformed data and enabling accurate analysis and decision-making.

# 5.3. Dynamic Column Creation based on Conditions

In the landscape of data transformation, the ability to dynamically create columns based on conditions opens up new avenues for insightful analysis. This chapter delves into advanced techniques for dynamically generating columns using conditional logic in Power Query. Through practical examples and step-by-step guidance, you'll learn how to harness the power of dynamic column creation to enhance your data transformation capabilities.

**Dynamic Column Creation:**

Dynamically generating columns empowers you to adapt your data to varying conditions, leading to more versatile and informative datasets.
```

Example:

Suppose you have a dataset containing sales records, and you want to dynamically calculate the total sales amount for each product based on their quantities and prices.

Step 1: Load Data

- Load the dataset containing sales records into Power Query.

Step 2: Create Dynamic Column

- Use the `Table.AddColumn` function to create a new column that calculates the total sales amount based on the quantity and price columns.

```M
let
    Source = YourSource,
    DynamicColumn = Table.AddColumn(Source, "Total Sales", each [Quantity] * [Price])
in
    DynamicColumn
```

Step 3: Load Data with Dynamic Column

- Load the dataset with the newly created "Total Sales" column into your destination.

Conditional Dynamic Column Creation:

Dynamically generating columns can also involve creating columns conditionally.

Example:

Consider a dataset containing customer ratings, and you want to create a dynamic column that categorizes customers as "Satisfied" or "Unsatisfied" based on a threshold rating.

Step 1: Load Data

- Load the dataset containing customer ratings into Power Query.

Step 2: Create Conditional Dynamic Column

- Use the `Table.AddColumn` function to create a new column that categorizes customers based on their ratings.

```M
let
    ThresholdRating = 4, // Set your threshold here
    Source = YourSource,
    CategorizeCustomers = Table.AddColumn(Source, "Satisfaction", each if [Rating] >= ThresholdRating then "Satisfied" else "Unsatisfied")
in
    CategorizeCustomers
```

Step 3: Load Data with Conditional Dynamic Column

- Load the dataset with the newly created "Satisfaction" column into your destination.

Multiple Conditional Dynamic Columns:

Creating multiple dynamic columns based on varying conditions can provide in-depth insights.

Example:

Suppose you have a dataset containing product sales data, and you want to create dynamic columns for each product category to show the total sales amount within that category.

Step 1: Load Data

- Load the dataset containing product sales data into Power Query.

Step 2: Create Multiple Conditional Dynamic Columns

- Use the `List.Distinct` function to extract unique product categories.

- For each category, use the `Table.AddColumn` function to create a dynamic column that calculates the total sales amount within that category.

```M
let
    Source = YourSource,
    Categories = List.Distinct(Source[Category]),
    AddSalesColumns = List.Accumulate(Categories, Source, (table, category) =>
      let
          FilteredRows = Table.SelectRows(table, each [Category] = category),
          TotalSalesColumn = Table.AddColumn(FilteredRows, "Total Sales " & category, each [Quantity] * [Price])
      in
```

```
            TotalSalesColumn

    )

in

    AddSalesColumns

```
```

Step 3: Load Data with Multiple Conditional Dynamic Columns

- Load the dataset with the newly created dynamic columns for total sales within each category into your destination.

Conclusion:

Dynamic column creation based on conditions is an advanced skill that empowers you to craft versatile and customized datasets. By mastering these techniques, you can adapt your data to changing circumstances and uncover insights that may be hidden in traditional column structures. Whether you're calculating totals, categorizing data, or creating custom views, dynamic column creation expands your data transformation capabilities. This chapter has equipped you with the tools to confidently implement advanced dynamic column creation, enabling you to generate tailored insights from your data and fueling more informed decision-making processes.
```

CHAPTER VI
Advanced Table Joins and Merging Techniques

6.1 Combining Data from Multiple Sources

The ability to combine data from multiple sources is fundamental for comprehensive analysis and decision-making. This chapter explores advanced techniques for joining and merging tables using Power Query, enabling you to create unified datasets from diverse data sources. Through practical examples and step-by-step guidance, you'll learn how to seamlessly integrate data to unlock deeper insights.

Understanding Table Joins:

Table joins involve merging data from different tables based on common columns, enriching your dataset with additional information.

Example:

Suppose you have two datasets: one containing customer information and the other containing transaction data. You want to combine these datasets to enrich the transaction data with customer details.

Step 1: Load Data

- Load both datasets containing customer information and transaction data into Power Query.

Step 2: Perform Inner Join

- Use the `Table.Join` function to perform an inner join between the two tables based on a common column (e.g., customer ID).

```M
let
    CustomerData = YourCustomerData,

    TransactionData = YourTransactionData,

    JoinedData = Table.Join(TransactionData, "CustomerID", CustomerData, "CustomerID", JoinKind.Inner)
in
    JoinedData
```

Step 3: Load Joined Data

- Load the merged dataset with enriched transaction data into your destination.

Merging Data from Different Sources:

Merging data from various sources, such as databases and CSV files, requires combining data from different file formats.

Example:

Imagine you have sales data stored in a CSV file and customer information in an Excel spreadsheet. You want to combine these datasets to analyze sales based on customer details.

Step 1: Load Data

- Load the CSV file containing sales data and the Excel spreadsheet containing customer information into Power Query.

Step 2: Perform Inner Join

- Use the `Table.Join` function to perform an inner join between the CSV and Excel tables based on a common column (e.g., customer ID).

```M
let

    SalesData = YourSalesData,

    CustomerData = YourCustomerData,

    JoinedData = Table.Join(SalesData, "CustomerID", CustomerData, "CustomerID", JoinKind.Inner)

in

    JoinedData
```

Step 3: Load Joined Data

- Load the merged dataset with sales data enriched with customer information into your destination.

Handling Different Join Types:

Different join types allow you to control how data is combined, whether you want to retain all records or only matching records.

Example:

Consider a scenario where you have a dataset of employees and another dataset of departments. You want to perform a left outer join to keep all employees while linking them to their respective departments.

Step 1: Load Data

- Load the datasets containing employee information and department details into Power Query.

Step 2: Perform Left Outer Join

- Use the `Table.Join` function to perform a left outer join between the employee and department tables based on a common column (e.g., department ID).

```M
let

    EmployeeData = YourEmployeeData,

    DepartmentData = YourDepartmentData,

    JoinedData    =    Table.Join(EmployeeData,    "DepartmentID",    DepartmentData,
"DepartmentID", JoinKind.LeftOuter)

in

    JoinedData

```

Step 3: Load Joined Data

- Load the merged dataset with employee data linked to their respective departments into your destination.

Conclusion:

Combining data from multiple sources is an advanced skill that empowers you to create comprehensive and informative datasets. By mastering these techniques, you can merge disparate data to uncover valuable insights and trends. Whether you're enriching data with related information, merging diverse file formats, or applying different join types, the ability to join and merge tables is a cornerstone of data integration and analysis. This chapter has equipped you with the tools to confidently implement advanced table joins and merging techniques, allowing you to create unified datasets that support in-depth analysis and decision-making processes.

6.2. Merging Strategies for Complex Data Sets

Working with complex data sets demands strategic merging techniques to maintain data integrity and glean accurate insights. This chapter delves into advanced strategies for merging tables in Power Query, providing you with the expertise to handle intricate data relationships and challenges. Through practical examples and comprehensive guidance, you'll learn how to navigate complex merging scenarios to unlock the full potential of your data.

Merging Hierarchical Data:

Complex data often includes hierarchical relationships, requiring specialized techniques for merging related data from different levels.

Example:

Imagine you have two datasets: one containing information about employees and another containing information about departments. The department dataset has a hierarchical structure with parent and child departments. You want to merge these datasets while maintaining the department hierarchy.

Step 1: Load Data

- Load the datasets containing employee information and hierarchical department data into Power Query.

Step 2: Perform Hierarchical Merge

- Use the `Table.NestedJoin` function to perform a hierarchical merge between the employee and department tables based on department IDs.

- Specify the hierarchical structure by creating a hierarchy definition using the `Table.AddColumn` function.

```M
let

    EmployeeData = YourEmployeeData,

    DepartmentData = YourDepartmentData,

    HierarchicalDepartment = Table.AddColumn(DepartmentData, "SubDepartments", each DepartmentData{[ParentDepartmentID= [DepartmentID]]}),

    MergedData = Table.NestedJoin(EmployeeData, "DepartmentID", HierarchicalDepartment, "DepartmentID", "DepartmentInfo")
in

    MergedData
```

Step 3: Load Merged Hierarchical Data

- Load the merged dataset with employee information enriched by hierarchical department data into your destination.

Handling Many-to-Many Relationships:

Dealing with many-to-many relationships requires advanced merging techniques to prevent data duplication and maintain accuracy.

Example:

Suppose you have a dataset with customers and another dataset with products. Both datasets have a many-to-many relationship, as customers can purchase multiple products, and products can be purchased by multiple customers. You want to create a bridge table that captures these relationships.

Step 1: Load Data

- Load the datasets containing customer and product information into Power Query.

Step 2: Create Bridge Table

- Use the `Table.Join` function to perform an inner join between the customer and product tables, creating a temporary table that captures customer-product relationships.

```M
let
    CustomerData = YourCustomerData,
    ProductData = YourProductData,
    BridgeTable = Table.Join(CustomerData, "CustomerID", ProductData, "CustomerID")
in
    BridgeTable
```

Step 3: Load Bridge Table

- Load the bridge table capturing the many-to-many relationships between customers and products into your destination.

Managing Data Duplication in Merge:

Handling data duplication during merges is crucial for maintaining accurate results and preventing overrepresentation.

Example:

Consider a scenario where you have a dataset of products and another dataset of suppliers. Some products are supplied by multiple suppliers, and you want to merge these datasets while avoiding duplicate products.

Step 1: Load Data

- Load the datasets containing product and supplier information into Power Query.

Step 2: Remove Duplicates

- Use the `Table.Distinct` function to remove duplicate products from the product dataset.

```M
let

    ProductData = YourProductData,

    DistinctProducts = Table.Distinct(ProductData, {"ProductID"})

in

    DistinctProducts
```

Step 3: Perform Merge with Deduplicated Data

- Use the deduplicated product dataset in the merge with the supplier dataset to avoid data duplication.

Conclusion:

Merging strategies for complex data sets require advanced techniques to address hierarchical relationships, many-to-many connections, and data duplication. By mastering these strategies, you can confidently navigate intricate data scenarios and create merged datasets that maintain accuracy and integrity. Whether you're merging hierarchies, handling many-to-many relationships, or deduplicating data, advanced merging techniques are essential for comprehensive data integration and analysis. This chapter equips you with the tools to effectively implement advanced merging strategies, enabling you to unlock deeper insights from your complex data sets and make informed decisions based on accurate information.

6.3. Joining Tables with Different Granularities

Merging tables with different levels of granularity requires specialized techniques to harmonize disparate data and draw meaningful insights. This chapter explores advanced strategies for joining tables with varying levels of detail using Power Query. Through practical examples and step-by-step instructions, you'll learn how to seamlessly integrate data from different granularities to gain a holistic perspective on your data.

Understanding Granularity in Data:

Granularity refers to the level of detail in data, such as daily, monthly, or yearly aggregates. Merging tables with different granularities necessitates careful consideration to ensure accurate analysis.

Example:

Suppose you have two datasets: one containing daily sales data and another containing monthly budget data. You want to combine these datasets to compare daily sales against monthly budgets.

Step 1: Load Data

- Load both datasets containing daily sales data and monthly budget data into Power Query.

Step 2: Aggregate Daily Sales to Monthly Level

- Use the `Table.Group` function to aggregate the daily sales data to the monthly level, summing up sales for each month.

```M
let

    DailySalesData = YourDailySalesData,

    MonthlySales = Table.Group(DailySalesData, {"Year", "Month"}, {{"Total Sales", each List.Sum([Sales]), type number}})

in

    MonthlySales

```

Step 3: Perform Join with Monthly Budgets

- Use the `Table.Join` function to perform an inner join between the aggregated monthly sales data and the monthly budget data based on the year and month columns.

```M
let
```

MonthlySalesData = YourMonthlySalesData,

MonthlyBudgetData = YourMonthlyBudgetData,

JoinedData = Table.Join(MonthlySalesData, {"Year", "Month"}, MonthlyBudgetData, {"Year", "Month"}, JoinKind.Inner)

in

JoinedData

```

**Step 4:** Load Joined Data

- Load the merged dataset with aggregated monthly sales data and monthly budget data into your destination.

**Dealing with Uneven Granularity:**

When joining tables with uneven granularity, such as combining weekly and monthly data, careful alignment is essential to prevent skewed insights.

**Example:**

Consider a scenario where you have weekly sales data and monthly marketing campaign data. You want to join these datasets while addressing the uneven granularity.

**Step 1:** Load Data

- Load the datasets containing weekly sales data and monthly marketing campaign data into Power Query.

**Step 2:** Align Weekly Data to Monthly Level
```

- Use the `Table.AddColumn` function to add a new column that calculates the corresponding month for each week in the weekly sales data.

```M
let

    WeeklySalesData = YourWeeklySalesData,

    WeeklyToMonthly    =    Table.AddColumn(WeeklySalesData,    "Month",    each
Date.StartOfMonth([Week Start Date]))

in

    WeeklyToMonthly

```

Step 3: Perform Join with Monthly Marketing Data

- Use the `Table.Join` function to perform an inner join between the weekly sales data aligned to the monthly level and the monthly marketing campaign data based on the year and month columns.

```M
let

    AlignedWeeklySalesData = YourAlignedWeeklySalesData,

    MonthlyMarketingData = YourMonthlyMarketingData,

    JoinedData    =    Table.Join(AlignedWeeklySalesData,    {"Year",    "Month"},
MonthlyMarketingData, {"Year", "Month"}, JoinKind.Inner)

in

    JoinedData

```

Step 4: Load Joined Data

- Load the merged dataset with weekly sales data aligned to the monthly level and monthly marketing campaign data into your destination.

Conclusion:

Joining tables with different granularities is an advanced skill that empowers you to draw insights from data of varying levels of detail. By mastering these techniques, you can harmonize data with different timeframes and levels of aggregation to create a comprehensive view. Whether you're aggregating data to match granularity, addressing uneven granularity, or aligning timeframes, advanced merging strategies are crucial for accurate analysis. This chapter equips you with the expertise to confidently implement advanced merging techniques for tables with different granularities, enabling you to uncover meaningful patterns and correlations within your data and make informed decisions based on comprehensive insights.

CHAPTER VII
Aggregating and Grouping Data Effectively

7.1 Aggregation Beyond Basic Functions

Aggregating and summarizing data is a cornerstone of data analysis, allowing you to distill complex information into meaningful insights. This chapter explores advanced aggregation techniques in Power Query, enabling you to perform comprehensive analysis by going beyond basic aggregation functions. Through practical examples and step-by-step guidance, you'll learn how to unleash the full potential of your data through advanced aggregation.

Understanding Advanced Aggregation:

Advanced aggregation techniques involve performing complex calculations on groups of data to extract valuable insights.

Example:

Suppose you have a dataset of customer reviews for different products. You want to calculate the average review score, along with the standard deviation and the number of reviews for each product.

Step 1: Load Data

- Load the dataset containing customer reviews and product information into Power Query.

Step 2: Perform Advanced Aggregation

- Use the `Table.Group` function to group the data by product and calculate the average, standard deviation, and count of reviews for each product.

```M
let
    ReviewData = YourReviewData,
    AggregatedData = Table.Group(ReviewData, "ProductID", {
        {"Average Score", each List.Average([ReviewScore]), type number},
        {"Standard Deviation", each List.StandardDeviation([ReviewScore]), type number},
        {"Review Count", each Table.RowCount(_), type number}
    })
in
    AggregatedData
```

Step 3: Load Aggregated Data

- Load the aggregated dataset with the calculated metrics for each product into your destination.

Aggregation with Custom Functions:

Custom aggregation functions allow you to perform specialized calculations tailored to your analysis.

Example:

Consider a dataset containing sales data for different products. You want to calculate the weighted average sale price, considering both the sale price and the quantity sold for each product.

Step 1: Load Data

- Load the dataset containing sales data and product information into Power Query.

Step 2: Create Custom Aggregation Function

- Define a custom aggregation function that calculates the weighted average based on sale price and quantity.

- Use the `Table.AggregateTableColumn` function to apply the custom aggregation function to the sales data.

```M
let
    SalesData = YourSalesData,
    WeightedAverage = (table) =>
        let
            TotalQuantity = List.Sum(table[Quantity]),
            WeightedSum = List.Sum(Table.AddColumn(table, "Weighted", each [SalePrice] * [Quantity])[Weighted]),
            WeightedAverage = if TotalQuantity <> 0 then WeightedSum / TotalQuantity else null
        in
            WeightedAverage,
    AggregatedData = Table.AggregateTableColumn(SalesData, "ProductID", {{"Weighted Average Sale Price", WeightedAverage}})
in
    AggregatedData
```

Step 3: Load Aggregated Data with Custom Aggregation

- Load the aggregated dataset with the calculated weighted average sale price for each product into your destination.

Aggregating by Multiple Columns:

Performing aggregation across multiple columns provides a comprehensive view of your data's characteristics.

Example:

Suppose you have a dataset of sales data with product categories and regions. You want to calculate the total sales amount for each combination of category and region.

Step 1: Load Data

- Load the dataset containing sales data, product categories, and regions into Power Query.

Step 2: Perform Aggregation by Multiple Columns

- Use the `Table.Group` function to group the data by both product category and region.

- Calculate the total sales amount for each group.

```M
let
    SalesData = YourSalesData,

    AggregatedData = Table.Group(SalesData, {"ProductCategory", "Region"}, {{"Total Sales",
each List.Sum([SalesAmount]), type number}})
```

in

AggregatedData

```
```

Step 3: Load Aggregated Data by Multiple Columns

- Load the aggregated dataset with the calculated total sales amount for each combination of product category and region into your destination.

Conclusion:

Aggregation beyond basic functions empowers you to extract deeper insights from your data, enabling more informed decision-making. By mastering these techniques, you can perform advanced calculations, create custom aggregation functions, and analyze data across multiple dimensions. Whether you're calculating averages, using custom functions, or aggregating data by multiple columns, advanced aggregation is a critical skill for gaining a comprehensive understanding of your data. This chapter equips you with the expertise to effectively implement advanced aggregation techniques, allowing you to uncover hidden trends, patterns, and correlations within your data and make informed decisions based on comprehensive insights.

7.2. Advanced Grouping and Summarizing Techniques

Effective data aggregation and summarization are essential for gaining insights from complex datasets. This chapter delves into advanced grouping and summarizing techniques using Power Query, allowing you to perform in-depth analysis and uncover valuable patterns. Through detailed examples and step-by-step instructions, you'll learn how to harness the power of advanced grouping and summarizing to extract meaningful insights from your data.

Understanding Advanced Grouping:

Advanced grouping involves creating custom groups based on specific criteria, enabling you to perform tailored analysis on subsets of your data.

Example:

Suppose you have a sales dataset with multiple product categories, and you want to analyze the top-selling product within each category.

Step 1: Load Data

- Load the sales dataset containing product categories and sales information into Power Query.

Step 2: Perform Advanced Grouping

- Use the `Table.Group` function to group the data by product category.

- Within each group, use the `Table.Max` function to find the record with the highest sales amount.

```M
let
    SalesData = YourSalesData,
    GroupedData = Table.Group(SalesData, "ProductCategory", {
        {"Top Selling Product", each Table.Max(_, "SalesAmount")}
    })
in
    GroupedData
```

Step 3: Load Grouped Data

- Load the grouped dataset with the top-selling product within each product category into your destination.

Custom Summarization with Advanced Techniques:

Custom summarization techniques allow you to extract specific insights from your data beyond basic aggregation functions.

Example:

Consider a dataset with customer transactions and the payment methods used. You want to calculate the percentage of each payment method's contribution to the total revenue.

Step 1: Load Data

- Load the dataset containing customer transactions and payment method information into Power Query.

Step 2: Perform Custom Summarization

- Use the `Table.Group` function to group the data by payment method.

- Calculate the total revenue for each payment method using the `List.Sum` function.

- Calculate the percentage contribution of each payment method to the total revenue.

```M
let
    TransactionData = YourTransactionData,
    GroupedData = Table.Group(TransactionData, "PaymentMethod", {
        {"Total Revenue", each List.Sum([Revenue]), type number},
```

{"Percentage of Total", each [Total Revenue] / List.Sum(TransactionData[Revenue]), type number}

  })

in

  GroupedData

```

**Step 3:** Load Summarized Data

- Load the summarized dataset with the total revenue and percentage contribution for each payment method into your destination.

**Hierarchical Summarization:**

Hierarchical summarization allows you to create multi-level summaries for in-depth analysis.

**Example:**

Suppose you have a dataset of sales data with product categories and subcategories. You want to calculate the total sales for each product category, along with the total sales for each subcategory within each category.

**Step 1:** Load Data

- Load the sales dataset containing product categories, subcategories, and sales information into Power Query.

**Step 2:** Perform Hierarchical Summarization

- Use the `Table.Group` function to group the data by both product category and subcategory.
```

- Calculate the total sales for each group.

```M
let
    SalesData = YourSalesData,
    GroupedData = Table.Group(SalesData, {"ProductCategory", "Subcategory"}, {
        {"Total Sales", each List.Sum([SalesAmount]), type number}
    })
in
    GroupedData
```

Step 3: Load Hierarchical Summarized Data

- Load the hierarchical summarized dataset with the total sales for each product subcategory within each product category into your destination.

Conclusion:

Advanced grouping and summarizing techniques empower you to extract nuanced insights from your data, enabling more informed decision-making. By mastering these techniques, you can create custom groups, perform custom summarizations, and analyze data hierarchically. Whether you're analyzing top-selling products, calculating percentage contributions, or creating hierarchical summaries, advanced grouping and summarizing skills are essential for gaining a deeper understanding of your data. This chapter equips you with the expertise to effectively implement advanced grouping and summarizing techniques, enabling you to uncover intricate trends, patterns, and relationships within your data and make well-informed decisions based on comprehensive insights.

7.3. Creating Custom Hierarchical Aggregations

Creating custom hierarchical aggregations in Power Query allows you to derive insightful summaries from hierarchical data structures. This chapter explores advanced techniques for building customized hierarchical aggregations, enabling you to analyze nested data with precision. Through concrete examples and step-by-step instructions, you'll learn how to harness the full potential of custom hierarchical aggregations to extract meaningful insights from complex datasets.

Understanding Hierarchical Aggregations:

Hierarchical aggregations involve summarizing data at multiple levels within a hierarchy, offering a comprehensive view of nested relationships.

Example:

Imagine you have a dataset containing sales data with information about regions, countries, and products. You want to create a custom hierarchical aggregation to calculate the total sales for each product at both the country and regional levels.

Step 1: Load Data

- Load the sales dataset with region, country, and product information into Power Query.

Step 2: Define Hierarchical Aggregation

- Define a custom aggregation function that calculates the total sales for a specific product at different hierarchy levels.

- Use the `Table.AggregateTableColumn` function to apply the custom aggregation function to the sales data.

```M
let
    SalesData = YourSalesData,
    HierarchicalAggregation = (table) =>
        let
            RegionalSales = List.Sum(table[SalesAmount]),
            CountrySales    =    Table.Group(table,    "Country",    {{"CountrySales",    each List.Sum([SalesAmount]), type number}})
        in
            Table.FromRecords({[Region    =    "Total",    Country    =    "Total",    Product    = table{0}[Product], CountrySales = RegionalSales]} & CountrySales),
    AggregatedData    =    Table.AggregateTableColumn(SalesData,    "Product", {{"HierarchicalAggregation", HierarchicalAggregation}})
in
    AggregatedData
```

Step 3: Load Custom Hierarchical Aggregation

- Load the dataset with the custom hierarchical aggregation, providing total sales for each product at both the country and regional levels.

Aggregating with Custom Groupings:

Creating custom groupings within hierarchical aggregations allows you to tailor your analysis to specific subsets of data.

Example:

Suppose you have a dataset of employee performance with hierarchical information about departments and teams. You want to create a custom hierarchical aggregation that calculates the average performance score for each team within each department.

Step 1: Load Data

- Load the employee performance dataset containing department, team, and performance information into Power Query.

Step 2: Define Custom Groupings for Hierarchical Aggregation

- Define a custom aggregation function that calculates the average performance score for teams within each department.

- Use the `Table.AggregateTableColumn` function to apply the custom aggregation function to the performance data.

```M
let
    PerformanceData = YourPerformanceData,
    HierarchicalAggregation = (table) =>
        let
            Department = table{0}[Department],
            TeamAverages = Table.Group(table, "Team", {{"Average Performance", each List.Average([PerformanceScore]), type number}})
        in
```

```
        Table.FromRecords({[Department = Department, Team = "Total", "Average
Performance" = List.Average(table[PerformanceScore])]} & TeamAverages),

    AggregatedData = Table.AggregateTableColumn(PerformanceData, "Department",
{{"HierarchicalAggregation", HierarchicalAggregation}})

in

    AggregatedData
```

Step 3: Load Custom Groupings Hierarchical Aggregation

- Load the dataset with the custom hierarchical aggregation, providing average performance scores for each team within each department.

Conclusion:

Creating custom hierarchical aggregations enables you to uncover nuanced insights from complex data structures, allowing for precise analysis of nested relationships. By mastering these techniques, you can build custom aggregations, tailor analysis to specific groupings, and derive meaningful insights from hierarchical data. Whether you're calculating totals at multiple levels or customizing groupings for analysis, advanced hierarchical aggregation skills are essential for gaining in-depth understanding of your data. This chapter equips you with the expertise to effectively implement custom hierarchical aggregation techniques, enabling you to extract valuable insights from intricate data structures and make well-informed decisions based on comprehensive insights.

CHAPTER VIII
Advanced Date and Time Transformations

8.1 Time Zone Conversion and Handling

In the realm of data manipulation, mastering advanced date and time transformations is crucial for accurate analysis. This chapter delves into the intricacies of time zone conversion and handling using Power Query. Through practical examples and step-by-step guidance, you'll learn how to effectively manage time zones, ensuring your data remains accurate and consistent across different regions and scenarios.

Understanding Time Zone Challenges:

Dealing with time zone differences is essential when working with data originating from various geographical locations. Incorrect handling can lead to skewed insights and inaccurate analysis.

Example:

Imagine you have a global sales dataset with timestamps recorded in different time zones. You want to convert all timestamps to a standardized time zone for consistent analysis.

Step 1: Load Data

- Load the sales dataset containing timestamps and geographical information into Power Query.

Step 2: Convert Time Zones

- Use the `DateTimeZone.SwitchZone` function to convert timestamps to the desired time zone. This function ensures that the time remains accurate even after conversion.

```M
let

    SalesData = YourSalesData,

    TargetTimeZone = DateTimeZone.FixedTimeZone(5), // Replace with your target time zone

    ConvertedData = Table.TransformColumns(SalesData, {"Timestamp", each DateTimeZone.SwitchZone(_, TargetTimeZone)})

in

    ConvertedData
```

Step 3: Load Converted Data

- Load the dataset with timestamps converted to the desired time zone for consistent analysis.

Handling Daylight Saving Time (DST):

Daylight Saving Time changes can complicate time zone handling. Properly accounting for DST is crucial for maintaining accurate data.

Example:

Suppose you have a dataset of flight departure and arrival times recorded in different time zones. You want to calculate the flight durations, considering any DST changes that might occur.

Step 1: Load Data

- Load the flight dataset containing departure and arrival times along with time zone information into Power Query.

Step 2: Calculate Flight Durations with DST Handling

- Use the `DateTimeZone.ToLocal` function to convert departure and arrival times to local time zones.

- Calculate the flight duration, considering any DST changes that might occur.

```M
let
    FlightData = YourFlightData,
    CalculateDuration = (departure, arrival, timeZone) =>
        let
            DepartureLocal = DateTimeZone.ToLocal(departure, timeZone),
            ArrivalLocal = DateTimeZone.ToLocal(arrival, timeZone),
            Duration = ArrivalLocal - DepartureLocal
        in
            Duration,
    ProcessedData = Table.AddColumn(FlightData, "Duration", each CalculateDuration([DepartureTime], [ArrivalTime], [TimeZone]))
in
    ProcessedData
```

Step 3: Load Processed Data

- Load the dataset with calculated flight durations, accounting for any DST changes.

Handling Irregular Time Intervals:

Sometimes, data might be recorded at irregular time intervals. Proper handling ensures accurate analysis.

Example:

Consider a dataset of sensor readings with irregular time intervals. You want to interpolate missing values to create a consistent time series.

Step 1: Load Data

- Load the sensor dataset containing timestamps and readings into Power Query.

Step 2: Interpolate Missing Values

- Use the `Table.FillDown` function to interpolate missing values in the dataset.

- This function propagates the last known value forward, creating a consistent time series.

```M
let
    SensorData = YourSensorData,
    InterpolatedData = Table.FillDown(SensorData, {"Reading"}, {"Timestamp"})
in
    InterpolatedData
```

Step 3: Load Interpolated Data

- Load the dataset with missing values interpolated, creating a consistent time series.

Conclusion:

Mastering advanced date and time transformations, particularly time zone conversion and handling, is essential for accurate data analysis. Whether dealing with time zone differences, Daylight Saving Time changes, or irregular time intervals, these techniques ensure your data remains reliable and consistent. This chapter equips you with the expertise to effectively implement advanced date and time transformation techniques, allowing you to accurately analyze data across different time zones and scenarios, make informed decisions based on precise insights, and maintain data integrity in complex scenarios.

8.2. Dealing with Irregular Time Intervals

Handling irregular time intervals in data analysis is a crucial skill that ensures accurate insights and proper interpretation of trends. This chapter explores advanced techniques for managing and analyzing data with irregular time intervals using Power Query. Through practical examples and detailed instructions, you'll learn how to effectively work with irregularly spaced time data, enabling you to make informed decisions based on accurate analysis.

Understanding Irregular Time Intervals:

Irregular time intervals occur when data points are not uniformly spaced, which can complicate analysis and visualization.

Example:

Imagine you have a dataset of stock prices with timestamps that don't follow a regular time interval. You want to create a consistent time series with evenly spaced intervals for easier analysis and visualization.

Step 1: Load Data

- Load the stock price dataset with timestamps and price information into Power Query.

Step 2: Create Consistent Time Intervals

- Use the `List.Generate` function to create a list of evenly spaced time intervals.

- For each interval, find the nearest timestamp in the dataset and extract the corresponding price.

```M
let
    StockData = YourStockData,
    StartTime = List.Min(StockData[Timestamp]),
    EndTime = List.Max(StockData[Timestamp]),
    Interval = Duration.FromMinutes(15), // Define your desired interval duration
    TimeIntervals = List.Generate(
        () => StartTime,
        each _ <= EndTime,
        each _ + Interval,
        each _),
    ExtractPrice = (timestamp) =>
        let
```

ClosestTimestamp = List.Min(StockData[Timestamp], each Duration.From(_ - timestamp) >= Duration.FromMinutes(0)),

Price = Table.SelectRows(StockData, each [Timestamp] = ClosestTimestamp){0}[Price]

in

Price,

ProcessedData = Table.FromList(TimeIntervals, Splitter.SplitByNothing(), {"Timestamp"})

in

ProcessedData = Table.AddColumn(ProcessedData, "Price", each ExtractPrice([Timestamp]))

in

ProcessedData

```

**Step 3:** Load Processed Data

- Load the dataset with evenly spaced time intervals and the corresponding extracted prices.

**Interpolating Missing Values in Irregular Data:**

Interpolating missing values is crucial for maintaining data consistency and enabling accurate analysis.

**Example:**

Suppose you have a dataset of temperature readings with irregular timestamps. You want to interpolate missing temperature values to create a complete time series.
```

Step 1: Load Data

- Load the temperature dataset with timestamps and temperature readings into Power Query.

Step 2: Interpolate Missing Values

- Use the `Table.FillDown` function to interpolate missing temperature values.

- This function propagates the last known value forward, creating a continuous time series.

```M
let
    TemperatureData = YourTemperatureData,
    InterpolatedData = Table.FillDown(TemperatureData, {"Temperature"}, {"Timestamp"})
in
    InterpolatedData
```

Step 3: Load Interpolated Data

- Load the dataset with missing temperature values interpolated, creating a complete time series.

Conclusion:

Dealing with irregular time intervals is a crucial aspect of data analysis. Whether you're creating consistent time series or interpolating missing values, these techniques ensure accurate insights and reliable analysis. This chapter equips you with the expertise to effectively handle irregular time intervals using advanced Power Query techniques. By mastering these methods, you can create more meaningful visualizations, accurately interpret trends, and make informed decisions based on complete and consistent data.

8.3. Extracting and Analyzing Date Components

Extracting and analyzing date components is a fundamental skill in data analysis, enabling you to derive valuable insights from temporal data. This chapter explores advanced techniques for extracting and analyzing various date components using Power Query. Through concrete examples and step-by-step guidance, you'll learn how to uncover meaningful patterns and trends hidden within your data, allowing for more informed decision-making.

Extracting Date Components:

Extracting date components, such as year, month, day, and day of the week, is essential for identifying temporal patterns.

Example:

Suppose you have a dataset of customer transactions with timestamps, and you want to analyze the sales trends by year and month.

Step 1: Load Data

- Load the customer transaction dataset with timestamps and sales information into Power Query.

Step 2: Extract Year and Month

- Use the `Table.AddColumn` function to extract the year and month from each timestamp.

```M
let

    TransactionData = YourTransactionData,
```

```
    AddYearMonth        =      Table.AddColumn(TransactionData,      "Year",      each
Date.Year([Timestamp])),

    AddYearMonth        =      Table.AddColumn(AddYearMonth,      "Month",      each
Date.Month([Timestamp]))

in

    AddYearMonth
```

Step 3: Load Data with Extracted Components

- Load the dataset with additional columns for year and month extracted from timestamps.

Analyzing Date Components:

Analyzing date components allows you to uncover patterns, such as seasonal trends or day-of-week effects.

Example:

Consider a dataset of website traffic with timestamps, and you want to analyze the traffic patterns by day of the week.

Step 1: Load Data

- Load the website traffic dataset with timestamps and traffic information into Power Query.

Step 2: Analyze Day of the Week

- Use the `Table.Group` function to group the data by day of the week.

- Calculate the average traffic for each day of the week.

```M
let
    TrafficData = YourTrafficData,
    GroupedByDay = Table.Group(TrafficData, Date.DayOfWeekName([Timestamp]), {
        {"Average Traffic", each List.Average([Traffic]), type number}
    })
in
    GroupedByDay
```

Step 3: Load Analyzed Data

- Load the dataset with average traffic for each day of the week.

Calculating Time Intervals:

Calculating time intervals between dates is valuable for measuring durations or analyzing trends.

Example:

Suppose you have a dataset of project tasks with start and end dates, and you want to calculate the duration of each task.

Step 1: Load Data

- Load the project task dataset with start and end dates into Power Query.

Step 2: Calculate Duration

- Use the `Table.AddColumn` function to calculate the duration of each task.

```M
let
    TaskData = YourTaskData,
    AddDuration = Table.AddColumn(TaskData, "Duration", each [EndDate] - [StartDate])
in
    AddDuration
```

Step 3: Load Data with Calculated Durations

- Load the dataset with additional column for calculated task durations.

Conclusion:

Extracting and analyzing date components is an essential aspect of temporal data analysis. Whether you're identifying temporal trends, analyzing day-of-week effects, or calculating time intervals, these techniques provide valuable insights into your data. This chapter equips you with the expertise to effectively extract and analyze date components using advanced Power Query techniques. By mastering these methods, you can uncover hidden patterns, trends, and relationships within your data, enabling you to make well-informed decisions based on comprehensive insights.

CHAPTER IX
Harnessing the Power of Custom Functions

9.1 Creating Custom Functions for Reusability

Creating custom functions in Power Query is a powerful way to enhance your data transformation workflow. This chapter delves into the art of designing and utilizing custom functions to achieve reusability and efficiency. Through practical examples and step-by-step guidance, you'll learn how to create, parameterize, and apply custom functions effectively, streamlining your data transformation process.

Understanding Custom Functions:

Custom functions encapsulate specific transformation logic, allowing you to apply the same operations across different datasets or scenarios.

Example:

Imagine you frequently encounter datasets with messy text data that needs cleaning. You want to create a custom function to remove special characters and convert text to lowercase.

Step 1: Define Custom Function

- Navigate to the "View" tab in Power Query Editor and select "Advanced Editor."

- Define your custom function using the M language.

```M
let
```

```
CleanText = (text) =>

  let

    CleanedText = Text.RemoveSpecialCharacters(Text.Lower(text))

  in

    CleanedText

in

  CleanText

```
```

Step 2: Create Custom Column

- In Power Query Editor, select the column containing messy text.

- Add a custom column using your created custom function.

Step 3: Apply Custom Function

- Load the data with the new custom column.

Parameterizing Custom Functions:

Parameterizing custom functions enhances their flexibility by allowing you to adapt their behavior based on input values.

Example:

Consider a scenario where you need to calculate sales tax based on different tax rates. You want to create a parameterized custom function to handle this.
```

Step 1: Define Parameterized Function

- In the "Advanced Editor," define your parameterized custom function using the M language.

```M
let
    CalculateSalesTax = (amount, taxRate) =>
        let
            Tax = amount * taxRate
        in
            Tax
in
    CalculateSalesTax
```

Step 2: Use Custom Function

- In Power Query Editor, create a custom column or transform an existing column using the parameterized custom function.

Step 3: Apply Custom Function with Parameters

- Load the data with the calculated sales tax using the parameterized custom function.

Advanced Function Techniques: Recursive and Iterative:

Advanced techniques like recursion and iteration in custom functions can solve complex data transformation challenges.

Example:

Suppose you have a hierarchical dataset representing an organization's structure. You want to create a custom function to calculate the total number of employees across all levels.

Step 1: Define Recursive Function

- In the "Advanced Editor," define a recursive custom function using the M language.

```M
let
    CalculateTotalEmployees = (employee, hierarchy) =>
        let
            DirectReports = Table.SelectRows(hierarchy, each [Manager] = employee),
            Subordinates = Table.SelectColumns(DirectReports, {"Employee"}),
            TotalSubordinates        =        Table.RowCount(Subordinates)        +
List.Sum(List.Transform(Table.ToRecords(Subordinates),                        each
CalculateTotalEmployees([Employee], hierarchy)))
        in
            TotalSubordinates
in
    CalculateTotalEmployees
```

Step 2: Apply Recursive Custom Function

- Create a custom column using the recursive custom function to calculate the total number of employees for each employee.

Step 3: Load Data with Calculated Totals

- Load the data with the calculated total number of employees for each employee.

Conclusion:

Creating custom functions in Power Query empowers you to achieve reusability, parameterization, and advanced transformation techniques. This chapter equips you with the skills to design and apply custom functions effectively, enhancing the efficiency of your data transformation workflow. By mastering the art of creating custom functions, you'll be able to tackle diverse data transformation challenges and achieve consistency, accuracy, and flexibility in your analyses and decisions.

9.2. Parameterized Functions for Dynamic Transformations

Parameterized functions in Power Query provide a dynamic and adaptable way to perform transformations on your data. This chapter dives into the world of parameterized functions, demonstrating their versatility in achieving dynamic transformations. Through concrete examples and step-by-step instructions, you'll learn how to create, utilize, and modify parameterized functions, enhancing your data transformation capabilities.

Understanding Parameterized Functions:

Parameterized functions allow you to pass external values to customize transformations, making your workflows more adaptable to varying scenarios.

Example:

Consider a dataset containing product prices in different currencies. You want to create a parameterized function to convert prices to a target currency based on exchange rates.

Step 1: Define Parameterized Function

- In Power Query Editor, navigate to the "View" tab and select "Advanced Editor."

- Create a parameterized function using the M language, including parameters for the exchange rate and target currency.

```M
let
    ConvertCurrency = (price, exchangeRate, targetCurrency) =>
        let
            ConvertedPrice = price * exchangeRate
        in
            Currency.FromText(targetCurrency) & Text.From(ConvertedPrice)
in
    ConvertCurrency
```

Step 2: Use Parameterized Function

- Apply the parameterized function to a column containing product prices, providing the exchange rate and target currency as parameters.

Step 3: Load Data with Converted Prices

- Load the data with the converted prices in the target currency.

Dynamic Column Transformation:

Parameterized functions enable dynamic column transformations based on external values.

Example:

Suppose you have a dataset of temperature readings in Fahrenheit, and you want to create a parameterized function to convert temperatures to Celsius.

Step 1: Define Parameterized Function

- In the "Advanced Editor," define a parameterized function for temperature conversion using the M language.

```M
let
    ConvertToFahrenheit = (temperature, toCelsius) =>
        let
            ConvertedTemperature = if toCelsius then (temperature - 32) * (5/9) else temperature
        in
            ConvertedTemperature
in
    ConvertToFahrenheit
```

Step 2: Use Parameterized Function

- Apply the parameterized function to a column containing temperature readings, specifying whether to convert to Celsius or not.

Step 3: Load Data with Converted Temperatures

- Load the data with the converted temperatures.

Hierarchical Transformations:

Parameterized functions are invaluable for hierarchical transformations where logic varies across levels.

Example:

Consider a dataset of sales with different tax rates for various products. You want to create a parameterized function to calculate the final price after applying tax.

Step 1: Define Parameterized Function

- In the "Advanced Editor," define a parameterized function for calculating final price using the M language.

```M
let
    CalculateFinalPrice = (price, taxRate) =>
        let
            FinalPrice = price * (1 + taxRate)
        in
            FinalPrice
in
    CalculateFinalPrice
```

Step 2: Use Parameterized Function

- Apply the parameterized function to a column containing product prices, providing the respective tax rate.

Step 3: Load Data with Calculated Final Prices

- Load the data with the calculated final prices after applying tax.

Conclusion:

Parameterized functions in Power Query unlock dynamic transformations, allowing you to adapt your data processing to varying conditions and requirements. This chapter equips you with the skills to create, use, and modify parameterized functions effectively, enhancing your data transformation capabilities. By mastering parameterized functions, you'll be able to streamline your workflows, achieve consistency in your analyses, and make data-driven decisions that account for dynamic factors and scenarios.

9.3. Advanced Function Techniques: Recursive and Iterative

Advanced function techniques, such as recursion and iteration, provide solutions to complex data transformation challenges. This chapter delves into the world of recursion and iteration in custom functions, showcasing their ability to solve intricate problems. Through concrete examples and step-by-step instructions, you'll learn how to harness these advanced techniques effectively, enhancing your data transformation capabilities.

Understanding Recursion:

Recursion is a powerful technique where a function calls itself to solve a problem that can be broken down into smaller instances of the same problem.

Example:

Imagine you have a hierarchical dataset representing an organization's structure. You want to create a custom function to calculate the total number of employees across all levels.

Step 1: Define Recursive Function

- In Power Query Editor, navigate to the "View" tab and select "Advanced Editor."

- Create a recursive function using the M language.

```M
let
    CalculateTotalEmployees = (employee, hierarchy) =>
        let
            DirectReports = Table.SelectRows(hierarchy, each [Manager] = employee),
            Subordinates = Table.SelectColumns(DirectReports, {"Employee"}),
            TotalSubordinates = Table.RowCount(Subordinates) + List.Sum(List.Transform(Table.ToRecords(Subordinates), each CalculateTotalEmployees([Employee], hierarchy)))
        in
            TotalSubordinates
in
    CalculateTotalEmployees
```

Step 2: Apply Recursive Function

- Create a custom column using the recursive custom function to calculate the total number of employees for each employee.

Step 3: Load Data with Calculated Totals

- Load the data with the calculated total number of employees for each employee.

Utilizing Iteration:

Iteration involves applying a function multiple times, each time using the result of the previous iteration.

Example:

Suppose you have a dataset of population growth rates for different countries. You want to create a custom function to calculate the population for multiple years based on the initial population and growth rates.

Step 1: Define Iterative Function

- In the "Advanced Editor," define an iterative function for population calculation using the M language.

```M
let
    CalculatePopulation = (initialPopulation, growthRate, years) =>
        let
            PopulationList = List.Generate(
                () => initialPopulation,
                each _ <= years,
                each _ * (1 + growthRate),
```

each _),

PopulationTable = Table.FromList(PopulationList, Splitter.SplitByNothing(), {"Population"})

in

PopulationTable

in

CalculatePopulation

```

**Step 2:** Use Iterative Function

- Apply the iterative custom function to calculate populations for different years.

**Step 3:** Load Data with Calculated Populations

- Load the data with the calculated populations for multiple years.

**Complex Data Transformations:**

Advanced techniques like recursion and iteration can handle complex data transformations that require step-by-step calculations.

**Example:**

Consider a dataset of financial transactions with varying transaction types. You want to create a custom function to calculate account balances for each transaction type.

**Step 1:** Define Complex Function
```

- In the "Advanced Editor," define a complex custom function for balance calculation using the M language.

```M
let
    CalculateBalance = (transactions, initialBalance) =>
        let
            ProcessedTransactions = List.Accumulate(
                transactions,
                {[TransactionType="Initial Balance", Amount=initialBalance]},
                (state, transaction) =>
                    let
                        PreviousBalance = List.Last(state)[Amount],
                        NewBalance = if transaction[TransactionType] = "Credit" then PreviousBalance + transaction[Amount] else PreviousBalance - transaction[Amount],
                        NewTransaction = [TransactionType=transaction[TransactionType], Amount=NewBalance]
                    in
                        state & {NewTransaction}),
            BalanceTable = Table.FromRecords(ProcessedTransactions)
        in
            BalanceTable
in
    CalculateBalance
```

Step 2: Use Complex Function

- Apply the complex custom function to calculate account balances for each transaction type.

Step 3: Load Data with Calculated Balances

- Load the data with the calculated account balances for each transaction type.

Conclusion:

Advanced function techniques, such as recursion and iteration, provide solutions to complex data transformation challenges. This chapter equips you with the skills to apply recursion and iteration in custom functions effectively, enhancing your data transformation capabilities. By mastering these advanced techniques, you'll be able to tackle intricate problems, handle complex calculations, and achieve accurate and insightful results in your data analyses.

CHAPTER X
Advanced Pivot and Unpivot Techniques

10.1 Handling Complex Pivot Transformations

Pivoting data is a powerful technique in data transformation, allowing you to reshape your data for better analysis and reporting. In this chapter, we'll explore advanced pivot techniques to handle complex transformation scenarios. Through detailed explanations and practical examples, you'll learn how to pivot data efficiently, accommodating various data structures and requirements.

Understanding Complex Pivot Transformations:

Complex pivot transformations involve reshaping data based on multiple columns and conditions, enabling you to derive valuable insights from intricate datasets.

Example:

Imagine you have a dataset containing sales data for different products, regions, and years. You want to pivot the data to create a summary table that shows total sales for each product in each year.

Step 1: Prepare the Data

- Load the raw sales data into Power Query Editor.

Step 2: Perform the Pivot Transformation

- Select the columns for product, year, and sales amount.

- In the "Transform" tab, click on "Pivot Column."

Step 3: Configure the Pivot Transformation

- In the Pivot Column dialog, select "Year" as the Pivot Column.

- Choose "Sum" as the Value Column and "Sales" as the Aggregate Value function.

Step 4: Load Data with Pivoted Table

- Load the pivoted table that displays total sales for each product in each year.

Handling Multiple Aggregations:

Complex pivot transformations often require applying multiple aggregation functions to different columns.

Example:

Consider the same sales dataset, but this time you want to pivot the data to show both total sales and average sales for each product in each year.

Step 1: Prepare the Data

- Load the raw sales data into Power Query Editor.

Step 2: Perform the Pivot Transformation

- Select the columns for product, year, sales amount, and average sales.

- In the "Transform" tab, click on "Pivot Column."

Step 3: Configure the Pivot Transformation

- In the Pivot Column dialog, select "Year" as the Pivot Column.

- Choose "Sum" as the Value Column and "Sales" as the Aggregate Value function.

- Add another aggregation: Select "Average" as the Value Column and "Average Sales" as the Aggregate Value function.

Step 4: Load Data with Multi-Aggregated Pivoted Table

- Load the pivoted table that displays both total and average sales for each product in each year.

Handling Missing Values:

Complex pivot transformations may result in missing values. Dealing with these gaps is essential for accurate analysis.

Example:

Suppose you have a dataset with missing sales data for some products in certain years. You want to pivot the data to show total sales for each product in each year, handling missing values appropriately.

Step 1: Prepare the Data

- Load the raw sales data into Power Query Editor.

Step 2: Perform the Pivot Transformation

- Select the columns for product, year, and sales amount.

- In the "Transform" tab, click on "Pivot Column."

Step 3: Configure the Pivot Transformation

- In the Pivot Column dialog, select "Year" as the Pivot Column.

- Choose "Sum" as the Value Column and "Sales" as the Aggregate Value function.

Step 4: Handle Missing Values

- In the pivoted table, you'll notice null values for missing sales data.

- Right-click on the column header with null values and select "Replace Values."

- Replace null values with zeros or appropriate placeholders.

Step 5: Load Data with Handled Missing Values

- Load the pivoted table with handled missing values.

Conclusion:

Advanced pivot transformations are essential tools for reshaping and analyzing complex datasets. This chapter has provided you with insights into handling intricate pivot scenarios efficiently. By mastering these techniques, you'll be well-equipped to reshape data for insightful analyses, tackle complex data structures, and derive valuable insights that aid in decision-making and reporting.

10.2. Unpivoting Multiple Columns with Custom Logic

Unpivoting data is a vital technique in data transformation that allows you to convert columns into rows, providing a clearer and more structured representation of your data. In this chapter, we will delve into the advanced technique of unpivoting multiple columns with custom logic. Through comprehensive explanations and hands-on examples, you will learn how to unpivot data efficiently while incorporating your own logic to handle complex scenarios.

Understanding Unpivoting Multiple Columns:

Unpivoting multiple columns involves transforming multiple related columns into a single column, providing a consolidated view of your data.

Example:

Imagine you have a dataset containing sales data for different product categories and regions, with separate columns for each year. You want to unpivot the data to create a structured representation where each row represents a specific year, product category, and region.

Step 1: Prepare the Data

- Load the raw sales data with separate columns for each year into Power Query Editor.

Step 2: Perform the Unpivot Transformation

- Select the columns for product category, region, and the year-specific sales columns.

- In the "Transform" tab, click on "Unpivot Columns."

Step 3: Configure the Unpivot Transformation

- In the Unpivot Columns dialog, select the year-specific sales columns as the columns to unpivot.

Step 4: Load Data with Unpivoted Table

- Load the unpivoted table where each row represents a specific year, product category, and region with corresponding sales.

Applying Custom Logic during Unpivoting:

Unpivoting with custom logic allows you to perform additional calculations or data manipulation during the transformation.

Example:

Suppose you have a dataset with sales data in different currencies for various product categories and regions. You want to unpivot the data and convert sales to a target currency based on exchange rates during the transformation.

Step 1: Prepare the Data

- Load the raw sales data with separate columns for each year and currency into Power Query Editor.

Step 2: Define Custom Logic

- In the "Advanced Editor," define a custom function to convert sales to a target currency based on exchange rates.

```M
let
    ConvertCurrency = (sales, exchangeRate) =>
        sales * exchangeRate
in
    ConvertCurrency
```

Step 3: Perform the Unpivot Transformation with Custom Logic

- Select the columns for product category, region, and the year-specific sales columns.

- In the "Transform" tab, click on "Unpivot Columns."

Step 4: Configure the Unpivot Transformation

- In the Unpivot Columns dialog, select the year-specific sales columns as the columns to unpivot.

Step 5: Apply Custom Logic during Unpivoting

- Apply the previously defined custom function to convert sales to the target currency based on exchange rates.

Step 6: Load Data with Unpivoted and Converted Sales

- Load the data with the unpivoted table containing sales converted to the target currency.

Handling Data Quality and Completeness:

Unpivoting multiple columns can uncover issues related to data quality and completeness. Addressing these issues is crucial for accurate analysis.

Example:

Consider a dataset with missing or incomplete sales data for various product categories and regions. You want to unpivot the data while handling missing values and ensuring data integrity.

Step 1: Prepare the Data

- Load the raw sales data with separate columns for each year into Power Query Editor.

Step 2: Perform the Unpivot Transformation

- Select the columns for product category, region, and the year-specific sales columns.

- In the "Transform" tab, click on "Unpivot Columns."

Step 3: Configure the Unpivot Transformation

- In the Unpivot Columns dialog, select the year-specific sales columns as the columns to unpivot.

Step 4: Handle Missing Values and Data Completeness

- In the unpivoted table, you'll notice null values for missing sales data.

- Right-click on the column header with null values and select "Replace Values."

- Replace null values with zeros or appropriate placeholders.

Step 5: Load Data with Handled Missing Values

- Load the data with the unpivoted table containing handled missing values.

Conclusion:

Unpivoting multiple columns with custom logic is a powerful technique that enables you to structure your data efficiently and apply specific calculations during transformation. This chapter has provided you with insights into handling intricate unpivoting scenarios effectively. By mastering these techniques, you'll be well-equipped to reshape data for analysis, address data quality challenges, and derive meaningful insights that support decision-making and reporting.

10.3. Creating Dynamic Pivot Tables with Power Query

Dynamic pivot tables are essential tools for handling evolving data structures and accommodating changing analysis requirements. In this chapter, we will delve into the advanced technique of creating dynamic pivot tables using Power Query. Through step-by-step explanations and practical examples, you will learn how to build versatile pivot tables that adapt to changing data, providing powerful insights for your analyses.

Understanding Dynamic Pivot Tables:

Dynamic pivot tables allow you to create pivot tables that automatically adjust to changes in data, such as new columns or rows.

Example:

Imagine you have a dataset containing sales data for different products and months. You want to create a dynamic pivot table that calculates total sales for each product in each month, regardless of the specific months present in the dataset.

Step 1: Prepare the Data

- Load the raw sales data with columns for product, month, and sales amount into Power Query Editor.

Step 2: Perform the Pivot Transformation

- Select the columns for product, month, and sales amount.

- In the "Transform" tab, click on "Pivot Column."

Step 3: Configure the Pivot Transformation

- In the Pivot Column dialog, select "Month" as the Pivot Column.

- Choose "Sum" as the Value Column and "Sales" as the Aggregate Value function.

Step 4: Load Data with Pivot Table

- Load the data with the pivot table that displays total sales for each product in each month.

Creating a Dynamic Pivot Table:

To create a dynamic pivot table, you'll utilize Power Query's features to adapt to changes in data automatically.

Step 1: Prepare the Data

- Load the raw sales data with columns for product, month, and sales amount into Power Query Editor.

Step 2: Build a Dynamic Pivot Table

- In the "Transform" tab, select "Pivot Column" to initiate the pivot transformation.

Step 3: Configure the Pivot Transformation

- In the Pivot Column dialog, select "Month" as the Pivot Column.

- Choose "Sum" as the Value Column and "Sales" as the Aggregate Value function.

Step 4: Handle Dynamic Data Changes

- As new months' data is added, Power Query will automatically update the pivot table to include the new months.

Step 5: Load Data with Dynamic Pivot Table

- Load the data with the dynamic pivot table that adjusts to changes in data over time.

Adapting to New Columns:

Dynamic pivot tables can also accommodate new columns, such as additional product categories, without manual adjustments.

Example:

Suppose you have a dataset containing sales data for different products and new product categories are added over time. You want to create a dynamic pivot table that includes new product categories without manual updates.

Step 1: Prepare the Data

- Load the raw sales data with columns for product, month, and sales amount into Power Query Editor.

Step 2: Build a Dynamic Pivot Table

- In the "Transform" tab, select "Pivot Column" to initiate the pivot transformation.

Step 3: Configure the Pivot Transformation

- In the Pivot Column dialog, select "Product" as the Pivot Column.

- Choose "Sum" as the Value Column and "Sales" as the Aggregate Value function.

Step 4: Handle New Product Categories

- As new product categories are added, Power Query will automatically update the pivot table to include the new categories.

Step 5: Load Data with Dynamic Pivot Table

- Load the data with the dynamic pivot table that adapts to new product categories.

Conclusion:

Creating dynamic pivot tables using Power Query empowers you to work with evolving data structures effortlessly. This chapter has equipped you with insights into building pivot tables that adjust to changes in data over time and new columns. By mastering these techniques, you'll be able to perform versatile analyses, adapt to data changes without manual intervention, and gain deeper insights that drive informed decision-making and reporting.

CHAPTER XI
Combining Power Query with Power BI and Excel

11.1 Integrating Power Query into Power BI Workflow

Integrating Power Query into the Power BI workflow is a seamless process that enhances data transformation and analysis capabilities. In this chapter, we will explore the integration of Power Query into Power BI, showcasing how to harness the synergy between these tools for more robust data processing and visualization.

Understanding the Power Query-Power BI Integration:

Power BI provides a unified platform for data visualization, and Power Query acts as the data preparation powerhouse, enabling you to shape and transform data before visualization.

Example:

Imagine you have a complex dataset containing sales data with multiple data quality issues. You want to create a Power BI report that visualizes clean and well-structured data, and you plan to use Power Query for data preparation.

Step 1: Connect to Data in Power BI

- Open Power BI Desktop.

- Click on "Get Data" to connect to your data source.

Step 2: Transform Data with Power Query

- Choose "Edit" to open Power Query Editor.

- Apply necessary data cleaning and transformation steps using Power Query functionalities.

Step 3: Load Transformed Data

- Click on "Close & Apply" to load the transformed data into Power BI.

Step 4: Build Visualizations

- Create visualizations in Power BI using the cleaned data.

Step 5: Refresh Data

- Whenever the source data changes, you can refresh the data in Power BI, and Power Query transformations will be applied automatically.

Utilizing Power Query's Transformations:

Power Query's advanced transformations are invaluable for data preparation before visualization in Power BI.

Example:

Suppose your dataset includes inconsistent date formats, missing values, and duplicated rows. You want to integrate Power Query's powerful transformations to clean the data before visualization.

Step 1: Connect to Data in Power BI

- Open Power BI Desktop.

- Click on "Get Data" to connect to your data source.

Step 2: Transform Data with Power Query

- Choose "Edit" to open Power Query Editor.

- Use transformations such as splitting columns, replacing missing values, and removing duplicates to clean the data.

Step 3: Load Transformed Data

- Click on "Close & Apply" to load the cleaned data into Power BI.

Step 4: Build Visualizations

- Create visualizations using the cleaned data.

Step 5: Refresh Data

- Refresh the data whenever needed, and the data transformations will be automatically applied.

Creating Custom Functions for Power BI:

Power Query's custom functions can be used in Power BI to streamline and reuse complex transformations.

Example:

Consider a dataset with textual data that requires intricate cleaning steps. You want to create a custom function in Power Query and use it in Power BI for consistent data preparation.

Step 1: Define Custom Function in Power Query

- In Power Query Editor, define a custom function that performs the required text cleaning.

```M
let
    CleanText = (text) =>
        Text.RemoveSpecialChars(text)
in
    CleanText
```

Step 2: Transform Data in Power BI using Custom Function

- In Power BI Desktop, follow the earlier steps to connect to data and transform it using the custom function.

Step 3: Load Transformed Data

- Click on "Close & Apply" to load the cleaned data into Power BI.

Step 4: Build Visualizations

- Create visualizations using the cleaned data.

Step 5: Refresh Data

- Refresh the data, and the custom function's transformations will be automatically applied.

Conclusion:

Integrating Power Query into the Power BI workflow amplifies your data preparation capabilities, ensuring clean, structured data for impactful visualizations. This chapter has demonstrated how to seamlessly integrate Power Query into Power BI, allowing you to leverage advanced transformations, create custom functions, and streamline your data preparation process. By mastering this integration, you'll enhance your ability to generate insightful reports and dashboards that empower data-driven decision-making.

11.2. Power Query Integration in Excel: Power Query Editor

Integrating Power Query into Excel through the Power Query Editor opens up a world of possibilities for data transformation and analysis within familiar Excel environments. In this chapter, we will explore the seamless integration of Power Query into Excel, focusing on how to harness the Power Query Editor for efficient data preparation and analysis.

Understanding Power Query Integration in Excel:

The Power Query Editor in Excel allows you to shape and transform data before loading it into your worksheets, enhancing data accuracy and enabling more sophisticated analyses.

Example:

Consider a scenario where you have a large Excel workbook containing multiple sheets of sales data with inconsistent formats. You want to clean and consolidate this data using Power Query Editor before performing analysis.

Step 1: Open Power Query Editor in Excel

- Open Excel.

- Navigate to the "Data" tab and click on "Get Data."

Step 2: Connect to Data Sources

- Choose the appropriate data source, such as an Excel file or external database.

- Select the specific sheets or tables you want to import.

Step 3: Transform Data with Power Query Editor

- Click on "Transform Data" to open Power Query Editor.

- Apply necessary transformations like data type conversion, merging tables, and filtering data.

Step 4: Load Transformed Data into Excel

- After transformations, click on "Close & Load" to load the cleaned data into your Excel workbook.

Step 5: Perform Analysis in Excel

- Utilize the transformed data for analysis and reporting within Excel.

Utilizing Advanced Transformations:

Power Query Editor's advanced transformations offer a wide range of options to cleanse and structure your data in Excel.

Example:

Suppose your dataset contains text data with inconsistent capitalization. You want to integrate Power Query Editor's advanced transformations to standardize the text case.

Step 1: Open Power Query Editor in Excel

- Open Excel.

- Navigate to the "Data" tab and click on "Get Data."

Step 2: Transform Data with Power Query Editor

- Choose the appropriate data source and select the data to import.

- Click on "Transform Data" to open Power Query Editor.

Step 3: Apply Advanced Transformations

- In Power Query Editor, use the "Text.Transform" function to convert text to lowercase or uppercase.

```M
let
    Source = ...,
    TransformText = Table.TransformColumns(Source, {"TextColumn", Text.Upper})
in
    TransformText
```

Step 4: Load Transformed Data into Excel

- After transformations, click on "Close & Load" to load the cleaned data into Excel.

Step 5: Perform Analysis in Excel

- Utilize the transformed data for analysis and reporting within Excel.

Creating Custom Functions in Power Query Editor:

You can create custom functions in Power Query Editor to automate complex data transformations and reuse them across your Excel workbooks.

Example:

Imagine you frequently work with datasets requiring the removal of special characters. You want to create a custom function in Power Query Editor to facilitate this process in Excel.

Step 1: Define Custom Function in Power Query Editor

- In Power Query Editor, define a custom function to remove special characters from a text column.

```M
let
    RemoveSpecialChars = (text) =>
        Text.RemoveSpecialChars(text)
in
    RemoveSpecialChars
```

Step 2: Apply Custom Function to Data

- Use the custom function on the text columns that need special character removal.

Step 3: Load Transformed Data into Excel

- After applying transformations, click on "Close & Load" to load the cleaned data into Excel.

Step 4: Perform Analysis in Excel

- Utilize the transformed data for analysis and reporting within Excel.

Conclusion:

Integrating Power Query Editor into Excel empowers you to refine and structure your data effortlessly before performing analyses or creating reports. This chapter has highlighted how to seamlessly integrate Power Query into Excel, utilizing its advanced transformations and custom function capabilities. By mastering this integration, you'll enhance your data preparation efficiency, improve data accuracy, and accelerate your Excel-based analytical workflows.

11.3. Sharing Queries Across Power BI and Excel

Sharing queries between Power BI and Excel provides a seamless and efficient way to maintain consistency in data transformations and analyses. In this chapter, we will explore the process of sharing queries across Power BI and Excel, showcasing how to leverage the synergy between these tools for streamlined data management and reporting.

Understanding Query Sharing Between Power BI and Excel:

Sharing queries enables you to reuse the same data transformations across different projects, ensuring consistency and reducing duplication of effort.

Example:

Imagine you have a set of complex data transformations applied to a dataset in Power BI. You want to reuse these transformations in an Excel workbook to ensure consistent data preparation.

Step 1: Prepare the Query in Power BI

- Open your Power BI project.

- Perform necessary data transformations using Power Query.

Step 2: Load the Query

- Click on "Close & Apply" to load the transformed data into Power BI.

Step 3: Export the Query

- In Power Query Editor, click on "Home" and then "Close & Apply."

- Choose "Close & Load To" and select "Only Create Connection" or "Add to Data Model."

Step 4: Import the Query into Excel

- Open Excel and navigate to the "Data" tab.

- Click on "Get Data" and choose the appropriate data source.

Step 5: Import Query from Power BI

- In the "Get Data" window, select "From Other Sources" and choose "Power Query."

- Browse to the Power BI file, select the query you want to import, and click "Import."

Step 6: Load the Query in Excel

- Click on "Close & Load" to load the query's connection into Excel.

Maintaining Consistency:

Sharing queries maintains consistency between Power BI and Excel, ensuring that the same transformations are applied to the data in both tools.

Example:

Suppose your Power BI project involves cleaning, transforming, and aggregating sales data. You want to replicate these transformations in Excel to keep your analyses aligned.

Step 1: Prepare the Query in Power BI

- Open your Power BI project.

- Apply the necessary data transformations using Power Query.

Step 2: Load the Query

- Click on "Close & Apply" to load the transformed data into Power BI.

Step 3: Export the Query

- In Power Query Editor, click on "Home" and then "Close & Apply."

- Choose "Close & Load To" and select "Only Create Connection" or "Add to Data Model."

Step 4: Import the Query into Excel

- Open Excel and navigate to the "Data" tab.

- Click on "Get Data" and choose the appropriate data source.

Step 5: Import Query from Power BI

- In the "Get Data" window, select "From Other Sources" and choose "Power Query."

- Browse to the Power BI file, select the query you want to import, and click "Import."

Step 6: Load the Query in Excel

- Click on "Close & Load" to load the query's connection into Excel.

Step 7: Maintain Consistency

- Whenever you refresh data in either Power BI or Excel, the same transformations will be applied, ensuring consistency in both tools.

Conclusion:

Sharing queries across Power BI and Excel streamlines data preparation and analysis processes, enhancing consistency and reducing duplicated efforts. This chapter has illustrated how to seamlessly share queries between these tools, enabling you to maintain uniformity in data transformations and analyses. By mastering this technique, you'll optimize your workflows, ensure data accuracy, and streamline your reporting across different platforms, ultimately empowering your decision-making processes.

CHAPTER XII
Performance Optimization and Best Practices

12.1 Optimizing Query Performance for Large Data Sets

Optimizing query performance is crucial when dealing with large data sets to ensure efficient data processing and analysis. In this chapter, we will delve into the strategies and best practices for optimizing query performance when working with substantial amounts of data.

Understanding Query Performance Optimization:

Large data sets can lead to slow query execution and resource-intensive operations. Optimizing query performance involves techniques that enhance data processing speed and reduce resource consumption.

Example:

Imagine you are working with a massive sales transaction dataset containing millions of records. You want to optimize the data retrieval and transformation process to ensure faster performance.

Step 1: Understand Data Requirements

- Define the specific data you need to retrieve and analyze.

- Avoid loading unnecessary columns or rows that don't contribute to your analysis.

Step 2: Filtering and Pagination

- Apply filtering conditions early in the query to reduce the data volume.

- Implement pagination techniques to retrieve data in smaller chunks, minimizing memory usage.

Step 3: Minimize Transformations

- Limit the number of complex transformations applied to the data.

- Use query folding whenever possible to push transformations back to the data source.

Step 4: Utilize Indexes and Constraints

- Leverage indexes and constraints in your data source to speed up data retrieval.

- Use WHERE clauses to take advantage of indexed columns for filtering.

Step 5: Data Types and Formats

- Use appropriate data types to reduce memory consumption.

- Avoid unnecessary data type conversions that can slow down the query.

Memory Management:

Optimizing memory usage is essential for efficient query performance, especially when dealing with large data sets.

Example:

Suppose you are processing a substantial dataset for sentiment analysis. You want to manage memory effectively to ensure smooth execution.

Step 1: Limit Data Loading

- Load only the required columns and rows for your analysis.

- Use the "Load more" option for Power Query transformations that involve large data sets.

Step 2: Divide and Conquer

- Split your analysis into manageable segments.

- Process each segment individually and combine results afterward.

Step 3: Clear Unused Objects

- Clear any intermediate or temporary tables used during data processing.

- Release memory by removing unnecessary objects from your environment.

Step 4: Close Unused Applications

- Close any other applications or processes that are consuming memory.

- This frees up resources for your data processing tasks.

Step 5: Monitor Resource Usage

- Keep an eye on memory and CPU usage during query execution.

- Optimize your process based on real-time resource consumption.

Parallel Processing:

Parallel processing can significantly enhance query performance by distributing tasks across multiple cores or nodes.

Example:

Consider a scenario where you are analyzing stock market data for multiple companies. You want to utilize parallel processing to speed up calculations.

Step 1: Divide Data into Chunks

- Split your data into smaller chunks or groups based on a specific criterion (e.g., companies).

- This creates subsets that can be processed in parallel.

Step 2: Parallelize Data Processing

- Use Power Query's parallel processing capabilities to process each chunk concurrently.

- This reduces the overall processing time.

Step 3: Combine Results

- Combine the results from each parallel task into a single output.

- Ensure that combining the results doesn't become a bottleneck.

Step 4: Monitor Performance

- Monitor the performance of parallel processing to ensure that it's speeding up the process.

- Adjust the chunk size and parallelism level if needed.

Conclusion:

Optimizing query performance for large data sets is essential for efficient data processing and analysis. This chapter has provided insights into techniques and best practices for enhancing query speed, minimizing memory consumption, and leveraging parallel processing. By applying these strategies, you'll be able to handle large data sets more effectively, reduce processing times, and achieve better overall performance in your data transformation and analysis tasks.

12.2. Query Folding: Maximizing Source Efficiency

Query folding is a critical concept for maximizing source efficiency and optimizing data transformation processes. In this chapter, we will explore the concept of query folding, its importance, and how to effectively implement it to improve query performance and minimize data processing overhead.

Understanding Query Folding:

Query folding refers to the process of pushing data transformation operations back to the data source whenever possible. Instead of processing transformations within the Power Query engine, query folding leverages the capabilities of the data source to execute transformations directly, resulting in faster and more efficient query execution.

Example:

Consider a scenario where you have a database with a large amount of customer transaction data. You want to perform filtering and aggregation operations efficiently by implementing query folding.

Step 1: Identifying Supported Transformations

- Understand which data source operations support query folding.

- Commonly supported operations include filtering, sorting, and aggregation.

Step 2: Applying Transformations in Power Query

- Use Power Query to apply data transformations.

- Ensure that the applied transformations can potentially be folded back to the source.

Step 3: Monitoring Query Folding

- Monitor query folding behavior during query execution.

- Power Query will attempt to fold operations back to the source where possible.

Step 4: Review Execution Plan

- Analyze the query execution plan to identify whether query folding occurred.

- The execution plan will indicate whether transformations were pushed down to the source.

Importance of Query Folding:

Query folding offers several benefits, including faster query execution, reduced data transfer, and efficient utilization of source capabilities.

Example:

Imagine you are working with a large CSV file containing sales data. By using query folding, you can filter and aggregate the data directly at the source, minimizing data transfer and optimizing performance.

Step 1: Filtering Data

- Apply filtering operations in Power Query to retrieve a subset of data.

- Ensure that the filtering operation can be folded back to the data source.

Step 2: Analyzing Query Execution

- Check the query execution plan to determine if the filtering operation was folded.

- If folded, the source will perform the filtering operation.

Step 3: Comparing Performance

- Measure the query execution time and resource consumption with and without query folding.

- You should observe improved performance with query folding.

Best Practices for Implementing Query Folding:

To effectively implement query folding, follow these best practices:

1. Choose Supported Operations: Focus on operations that are supported for query folding by the data source, such as filtering, sorting, and aggregation.

2. Minimize Data Transfer: Folded queries reduce data transferred between the source and Power Query, leading to improved performance.

3. Use Native Functions: Utilize native functions available in the source database for transformations whenever possible.

4. Avoid Complex Expressions: Keep transformations relatively simple to increase the likelihood of query folding.

5. Monitor Execution Plans: Regularly review query execution plans to ensure that folding is occurring as intended.

6. Testing and Profiling: Test query folding with different data scenarios and profile the performance impact.

Conclusion:

Query folding is a powerful technique for optimizing query performance by leveraging source capabilities. This chapter has demonstrated the significance of query folding, outlined its implementation steps, and provided best practices for its effective usage. By incorporating query folding into your data transformation workflows, you'll experience faster query execution, reduced data transfer, and improved overall efficiency in your data analysis tasks.

12.3. Data Loading and Refreshing Best Practices

Efficient data loading and refreshing are essential for maintaining accurate and up-to-date information in your analysis. This chapter delves into best practices for optimizing data loading and refreshing processes, ensuring that your data remains current while minimizing resource usage and improving overall performance.

Understanding Data Loading and Refreshing:

Data loading and refreshing involve bringing data into your analysis tool and updating it with the latest information from the source. Efficient data loading and refreshing practices are crucial for maintaining the timeliness and accuracy of your analysis.

Example:

Consider a scenario where you're working with a sales dashboard that requires frequent updates to reflect the latest sales data. You want to optimize the data loading and refreshing process to ensure real-time insights.

Step 1: Determine Data Refresh Frequency

- Define how frequently your data needs to be updated.

- Consider factors like business requirements and data source update frequency.

Step 2: Choose an Appropriate Data Source

- Choose a data source that supports the required refresh frequency.

- Some data sources offer real-time connections, while others may require scheduled refreshes.

Step 3: Schedule Data Refreshes

- Configure scheduled refreshes based on the determined frequency.

- Most analysis tools, like Power BI and Excel, allow you to set up automated refresh schedules.

Step 4: Optimize Data Queries

- Design your data queries to retrieve only the necessary data.

- Limit unnecessary columns and rows to reduce data transfer time.

Optimizing Data Loading and Refreshing:

Efficient data loading and refreshing contribute to better performance, reduced resource consumption, and accurate analysis results.

Example:

Suppose you are building a dashboard for monitoring website traffic. You want to ensure that the data loading and refreshing process is optimized for timely insights.

Step 1: Data Selection

- Select the relevant data sources for your analysis.

- Avoid selecting unnecessary data that doesn't contribute to your analysis.

Step 2: Data Transformation

- Apply necessary data transformations using Power Query or similar tools.

- Keep transformations optimized for speed and efficiency.

Step 3: Schedule Refresh

- Set up a refresh schedule that aligns with your business needs.

- Determine whether real-time refreshes or scheduled refreshes are more appropriate.

Step 4: Monitor Refresh Performance

- Monitor the performance of data loading and refreshing processes.

- Identify any bottlenecks or slowdowns and address them promptly.

Step 5: Avoid Unnecessary Refreshes

- Avoid refreshing data unnecessarily.

- Set up conditional refresh triggers based on changes in the source data.

Step 6: Manage Incremental Loading

- Implement incremental loading where applicable.

- Load only new or changed data since the last refresh to reduce data transfer.

Step 7: Data Compression

- Compress data where possible to reduce storage and transfer requirements.

- Utilize compression techniques available in your analysis tool.

Conclusion:

Efficient data loading and refreshing practices are essential for maintaining accurate and up-to-date analysis results. This chapter has provided insights into optimizing data loading and refreshing processes, from selecting the right data sources to scheduling refreshes and managing incremental loading. By following these best practices, you'll ensure that your analysis remains current, your insights are accurate, and your performance is optimized, ultimately enhancing your decision-making processes.

CHAPTER XIII
Advanced Data Cleansing and Enrichment

13.1 Handling Dirty Data: Advanced Cleaning Techniques

Dealing with dirty data—data that is inaccurate, incomplete, or inconsistent—is a common challenge in data analysis. This chapter explores advanced data cleansing techniques that go beyond basic cleaning methods. We'll delve into strategies for identifying and rectifying various types of data quality issues, ensuring that your analysis is based on reliable and accurate information.

Understanding Dirty Data:

Dirty data can stem from various sources, including human errors, system glitches, and data integration issues. Advanced data cleansing techniques are essential to address complex issues and ensure the integrity of your analysis.

Example:

Imagine you are working with a dataset containing customer information. The data is riddled with spelling errors, duplicate records, and missing values. You want to apply advanced cleaning techniques to prepare the data for analysis.

Step 1: Data Profiling

- Begin by profiling the data to identify common data quality issues.

- Use tools like Power Query to create summary statistics and identify anomalies.

Step 2: Identify Data Patterns

KIET HUYNH

- Identify patterns that indicate potential errors or inconsistencies.

- Look for patterns in names, addresses, dates, and other relevant fields.

Step 3: Leverage Regular Expressions

- Utilize regular expressions to identify and correct data inconsistencies.

- For instance, correct misspelled names or addresses using regex patterns.

Step 4: Handling Duplicate Records

- Identify duplicate records using a combination of fields.

- Develop a strategy to merge or eliminate duplicates while retaining relevant information.

Step 5: Filling Missing Values

- Use advanced techniques to fill missing values based on patterns and relationships.

- Predictive modeling or interpolation methods can be applied to fill gaps.

Step 6: Outlier Detection and Correction

- Identify outliers that could be erroneous data points.

- Decide whether to correct, remove, or investigate outliers based on the context.

Step 7: Addressing Inconsistent Formats

- Standardize inconsistent formats such as dates, currencies, and measurements.

- Apply consistent formatting rules across the dataset.

Data Enrichment:

Data enrichment involves enhancing your dataset by adding relevant external information. This process can improve the quality and depth of your analysis.

Example:

Suppose you're analyzing customer data and want to enrich it with additional demographic information.

Step 1: Identify Enrichment Sources

- Determine external sources that can provide the desired additional information.

- Look for publicly available data, APIs, or data providers.

Step 2: Extract External Data

- Use Power Query or other data integration tools to extract external data.

- Merge the external data with your existing dataset based on common identifiers.

Step 3: Data Alignment

- Ensure that the external data is aligned correctly with your dataset.

- Handle cases where identifiers might have different formats or spellings.

Step 4: Quality Check

- Assess the quality of the enriched data for accuracy and reliability.

- Validate external data sources before incorporating them into your analysis.

Step 5: Update and Refresh

- Establish a mechanism to update the enriched data periodically.

- Set up scheduled refreshes to keep the data current.

Conclusion:

Advanced data cleansing techniques are crucial for addressing complex data quality issues and enhancing the reliability of your analysis. This chapter has explored strategies for handling dirty data, including using regular expressions, addressing duplicates and missing values, detecting outliers, and enriching data with external sources. By implementing these techniques, you'll ensure that your analysis is based on accurate and trustworthy data, leading to more reliable insights and better decision-making.

13.2. Data Enrichment with Web Services and APIs

Data enrichment involves enhancing your dataset with additional information from external sources. Web services and APIs (Application Programming Interfaces) provide a powerful way to gather real-time and relevant data to complement your analysis. This chapter explores advanced techniques for leveraging web services and APIs to enrich your data, improving the quality and depth of your insights.

Understanding Data Enrichment with Web Services and APIs:

Web services and APIs allow you to access external data sources programmatically, fetching data in real-time and integrating it seamlessly into your analysis. This process can provide valuable context and enhance the understanding of your data.

Example:

Imagine you're working on a project analyzing social media engagement. You want to enrich your dataset with demographic information about the users engaging with your content.

Step 1: Identify Enrichment Needs

- Determine what additional information would enhance your analysis.

- In this case, you want to add demographic data such as age and location.

Step 2: Choose Relevant APIs

- Research and select APIs that provide the desired information.

- Social media platforms often offer APIs for retrieving user data.

Step 3: Register and Obtain API Keys

- Sign up for access to the chosen APIs and obtain API keys.

- API keys are required to authenticate your requests and track usage.

Step 4: Query the API

- Use programming languages like Python or tools like Power Query to query the API.

- Send requests with appropriate parameters to retrieve relevant data.

Step 5: Data Integration

- Integrate the API response with your existing dataset.

- Match API data with your data using unique identifiers like user IDs.

Step 6: Handle Rate Limits

- APIs often have rate limits to prevent abuse.

- Implement strategies to manage rate limits and ensure smooth data retrieval.

Step 7: Data Validation

- Validate API data for accuracy and consistency.

- Perform checks to ensure that the enriched data aligns with your analysis goals.

Example: Data Enrichment from Twitter API

Step 1: Identify Enrichment Needs

- Determine the Twitter handles for which you want to enrich data.

Step 2: Choose Twitter API

- Register a developer account with Twitter and create an application to obtain API keys.

Step 3: Query User Data

- Use Python and the Tweepy library to query the Twitter API for user data.

- Retrieve information such as follower count, location, and bio.

Step 4: Integrate Data

- Match the API data with your existing dataset using Twitter handles.

- Create a unique identifier for each Twitter handle in your dataset.

Step 5: Rate Limits and Error Handling

- Twitter API has rate limits, so implement rate limit handling and error retries.

- Store API responses and handle exceptions to ensure data integrity.

Step 6: Data Validation

- Validate enriched data for inconsistencies or missing values.

- Check if the retrieved follower count aligns with your expectations.

Conclusion:

Leveraging web services and APIs for data enrichment enhances the depth and quality of your analysis. This chapter has demonstrated how to identify enrichment needs, choose relevant APIs, query the APIs, integrate the data, handle rate limits, and validate the enriched information. By mastering these techniques, you can ensure that your analysis is enriched with accurate and up-to-date external data, leading to more comprehensive insights and better decision-making.

13.3. Implementing Data Validation and Quality Checks

Data validation and quality checks are essential steps in ensuring that your enriched dataset is accurate, reliable, and suitable for analysis. This chapter explores advanced techniques for implementing comprehensive data validation and quality checks, enabling you to identify and rectify potential issues before they impact your insights.

Understanding Data Validation and Quality Checks:

Data validation involves verifying the integrity of your data by assessing its accuracy, completeness, and consistency. Quality checks ensure that your data meets predefined standards and criteria, reducing the risk of erroneous conclusions.

Example:

Consider an e-commerce dataset containing customer orders. You've enriched the dataset with shipping addresses from an external source and want to ensure its accuracy.

Step 1: Define Validation Rules

- Define rules that your enriched data should adhere to.

- For addresses, rules could include valid postal codes and consistent city-state combinations.

Step 2: Validate Field Formats

- Use regular expressions or formatting functions to validate field formats.

- Ensure that dates, phone numbers, and other fields follow expected patterns.

Step 3: Cross-Field Validation

- Check for inconsistencies between related fields.

- Validate that the postal code matches the state and city, for instance.

Step 4: Detect Outliers and Anomalies

- Apply statistical methods to identify outliers or anomalies.

- Remove or investigate data points that deviate significantly from the norm.

Step 5: Data Completeness

- Verify that all required fields are present and populated.

- Address missing values before proceeding with analysis.

Step 6: Data Consistency

- Compare enriched data with your original dataset for consistency.

- Ensure that the added information aligns with your existing data.

Step 7: Custom Quality Metrics

- Define custom quality metrics based on your analysis goals.

- These could include data freshness, accuracy rates, or conformity to specific criteria.

Example: Data Validation for Enriched Addresses

Step 1: Define Validation Rules

- Specify rules for valid postal codes, state abbreviations, and city names.

Step 2: Validate Postal Codes

- Use regular expressions to validate the postal code format.

- Ensure that postal codes match the expected format for the given country.

Step 3: Cross-Field Validation

- Validate that the city and state combination is valid.

- Check whether the state corresponds to the selected city.

Step 4: Detect Missing Values

- Identify addresses with missing components.

- Consider enriching these addresses again or using fallback data.

Step 5: Data Consistency

- Compare enriched addresses with the original data.

- Ensure that the added information is consistent with the dataset.

Step 6: Custom Quality Metrics

- Calculate accuracy rates for the enriched addresses.

- Measure how many addresses conform to the defined validation rules.

Conclusion:

Implementing data validation and quality checks is crucial for ensuring that your enriched dataset is accurate and reliable. This chapter has demonstrated techniques for defining validation rules, validating field formats, cross-field validation, detecting outliers, ensuring data completeness, checking data consistency, and defining custom quality metrics. By incorporating these advanced validation methods into your data enrichment process, you can maintain data integrity and enhance the credibility of your analysis, leading to more robust insights and better decision-making.

CHAPTER XIV
Case Studies: Real-World Data Transformations

14.1 Financial Data Transformation and Analysis

In this chapter, we will delve into a real-world case study that focuses on the transformation and analysis of financial data. Financial data often comes in various formats and from multiple sources, making it crucial to employ advanced techniques for data integration, cleansing, and analysis. We will explore how to prepare and transform financial data for meaningful insights.

Case Study: Analyzing Financial Data for Investment Decisions

Step 1: Data Collection and Integration

- Gather financial data from different sources such as stock exchanges, financial statements, and economic indicators.

- Utilize Power Query to load and combine data from various sources into a single structured dataset.

Step 2: Data Cleansing and Validation

- Identify and handle missing values, outliers, and inconsistent data points.

- Validate the accuracy of financial metrics like revenue, expenses, and earnings.

Step 3: Currency Conversion

- If dealing with international data, perform currency conversion to ensure uniform analysis.

- Utilize exchange rate data from reputable sources or APIs for accurate conversions.

Step 4: Time Series Transformation

- Convert time-based data into a consistent time series format.

- Ensure uniform intervals and handle irregular data points appropriately.

Step 5: Calculation of Financial Metrics

- Calculate essential financial metrics like earnings per share (EPS), price-to-earnings (P/E) ratio, and return on investment (ROI).

- Utilize custom functions for complex calculations and aggregations.

Step 6: Trend Analysis and Visualization

- Visualize financial trends using line charts, bar graphs, and candlestick charts.

- Identify patterns and anomalies that could inform investment decisions.

Step 7: Forecasting and Predictive Analytics

- Utilize time series analysis techniques for forecasting future financial metrics.

- Apply methods like moving averages, exponential smoothing, or ARIMA models.

Example: Analyzing Stock Prices and Performance

Step 1: Data Collection and Integration

- Gather historical stock price data from stock exchange APIs.

- Import economic indicators like GDP growth and inflation rate from reliable sources.

Step 2: Data Cleansing and Validation

- Handle missing data by interpolating or using alternative data sources.

- Validate that stock prices align with the expected range for each company.

Step 3: Currency Conversion

- Convert stock prices listed in different currencies to a common base currency.

- Utilize currency exchange rates from financial data providers.

Step 4: Time Series Transformation

- Resample data to a consistent interval (e.g., daily or weekly).

- Fill in gaps in data caused by weekends or holidays.

Step 5: Calculation of Financial Metrics

- Calculate metrics like price-to-earnings (P/E) ratio and dividend yield.

- Create custom functions for intricate calculations involving market capitalization.

Step 6: Trend Analysis and Visualization

- Plot stock price trends and financial metrics over time.

- Identify correlations between economic indicators and stock performance.

Step 7: Forecasting and Predictive Analytics

- Apply time series forecasting to predict future stock prices.

- Utilize exponential smoothing methods for short-term predictions.

Conclusion:

The financial data transformation and analysis case study highlights the importance of handling diverse financial data effectively. By employing advanced Power Query techniques, such as data integration, cleansing, currency conversion, time series transformation, metric calculation, trend analysis, and forecasting, you can extract valuable insights for making informed investment decisions. This case study demonstrates the practical application of these techniques, underscoring their relevance in the financial domain and their potential to drive profitable outcomes.

14.2. Sales and Inventory Management Transformation

In this chapter, we will explore a practical case study involving the transformation of sales and inventory management data. Sales and inventory data are crucial for businesses to optimize their operations and make informed decisions. We will delve into how advanced Power Query techniques can be used to clean, transform, and analyze these datasets, ultimately leading to improved inventory management and strategic planning.

Case Study: Optimizing Sales and Inventory Management

Step 1: Data Collection and Integration

- Collect sales data from different sales channels such as online platforms, retail stores, and distribution centers.

- Integrate inventory data from warehouses to track stock levels.

Step 2: Data Cleansing and Validation

- Identify and handle missing or incorrect entries in sales and inventory records.

- Validate that product IDs, quantities, and prices align with business expectations.

Step 3: Data Aggregation and Summarization

- Aggregate sales data to different levels, such as daily, weekly, and monthly.

- Summarize sales quantities and revenues for each product and time period.

Step 4: Inventory Analysis

- Calculate inventory turnover ratios to assess how quickly products are sold.

- Analyze slow-moving and fast-moving products for optimized stocking.

Step 5: Identifying Seasonal Trends

- Utilize time series analysis to identify seasonal patterns in sales data.

- Adjust inventory levels based on predicted spikes or drops in demand.

Step 6: Replenishment Strategies

- Implement inventory replenishment strategies like Just-In-Time (JIT) or Economic Order Quantity (EOQ).

- Set reorder points and safety stock levels for efficient inventory management.

Step 7: Visualizing Sales and Inventory Insights

- Create visually informative dashboards to monitor sales and inventory trends.

- Visualize inventory turnover rates and stock levels over time.

Example: Enhancing Sales and Inventory Management

Step 1: Data Collection and Integration

- Collect sales data from point-of-sale systems and e-commerce platforms.

- Integrate inventory data from warehouses and distribution centers.

Step 2: Data Cleansing and Validation

- Handle missing data by imputing values or excluding affected records.

- Validate that product IDs and quantities are within reasonable ranges.

Step 3: Data Aggregation and Summarization

- Aggregate sales data on a weekly basis to understand weekly trends.

- Summarize sales quantities and revenues for each product and week.

Step 4: Inventory Analysis

- Calculate inventory turnover ratios for different product categories.

- Identify slow-moving products that may require discounts or promotions.

Step 5: Identifying Seasonal Trends

- Apply time series decomposition to identify seasonal patterns.

- Adjust inventory levels to accommodate higher demand during holidays.

Step 6: Replenishment Strategies

- Implement JIT for fast-moving products with consistent demand.

- Use EOQ for products with variable demand and lead times.

Step 7: Visualizing Sales and Inventory Insights

- Create a dashboard with line charts for sales trends and bar graphs for inventory levels.

- Monitor inventory turnover rates and stockout incidents.

Conclusion:

The sales and inventory management transformation case study demonstrates the practical application of advanced Power Query techniques for enhancing business operations. By collecting, integrating, cleansing, validating, aggregating, and analyzing sales and inventory data, organizations can gain valuable insights into their products' performance and optimize their inventory management strategies. This case study underscores the importance of data-driven decision-making and showcases how Power Query empowers businesses to make informed choices for better sales and inventory management outcomes.

14.3. Customer and Marketing Analytics Transformation

In this chapter, we will delve into a comprehensive case study that focuses on the transformation of customer and marketing data for actionable insights. Customer and marketing analytics play a pivotal role in understanding consumer behavior, optimizing marketing strategies, and enhancing customer experiences. Through this case study, we will explore how advanced Power Query techniques can be applied to clean, analyze, and derive valuable insights from customer and marketing datasets.

Case Study: Enhancing Customer and Marketing Analytics

Step 1: Data Collection and Integration

- Collect customer data from various touchpoints such as online interactions, purchases, and surveys.

- Integrate marketing data from different sources including social media, email campaigns, and website analytics.

Step 2: Data Cleansing and Validation

- Identify and handle inconsistencies in customer attributes like names, addresses, and contact information.

- Validate that marketing campaign data aligns with expected metrics and targets.

Step 3: Customer Segmentation

- Group customers into segments based on demographic, behavioral, or transactional attributes.

- Utilize clustering techniques to identify patterns and segments.

Step 4: Campaign Performance Analysis

- Analyze the effectiveness of marketing campaigns by measuring metrics like conversion rates, click-through rates, and ROI.

- Compare campaign performance across different channels and segments.

Step 5: Churn Prediction

- Build predictive models to identify customers at risk of churn (leaving) based on historical data.

- Utilize machine learning algorithms to predict churn probabilities.

Step 6: Personalization and Recommendation

- Implement personalization strategies by suggesting products or offers based on customer preferences and behaviors.

- Use collaborative filtering or content-based recommendations to enhance customer experiences.

Step 7: Visualizing Customer Insights

- Create interactive dashboards to visualize customer segments, campaign performance, and churn predictions.

- Visualize customer journeys and touchpoints to identify potential areas for improvement.

Example: Customer and Marketing Analytics Enhancement

Step 1: Data Collection and Integration

- Collect customer data including demographics, transaction history, and customer interactions.

- Integrate data from marketing campaigns such as email open rates, social media engagement, and website visits.

Step 2: Data Cleansing and Validation

- Standardize customer addresses and contact details using data cleansing techniques.

- Validate that marketing metrics like click-through rates align with campaign expectations.

Step 3: Customer Segmentation

- Group customers into segments based on their purchasing behaviors, preferences, and demographics.

- Use k-means clustering to create distinct customer segments.

Step 4: Campaign Performance Analysis

- Calculate conversion rates for different marketing channels and campaigns.

- Analyze which campaigns generated the highest ROI and engagement.

Step 5: Churn Prediction

- Build a churn prediction model using historical churn data and relevant features.

- Utilize logistic regression or decision trees to predict customers likely to churn.

Step 6: Personalization and Recommendation

- Recommend products to customers based on their previous purchases and browsing history.

- Implement collaborative filtering to recommend products based on similar customers' preferences.

Step 7: Visualizing Customer Insights

- Create a dashboard showcasing customer segments, campaign performance metrics, and churn predictions.

- Visualize customer journeys to identify drop-off points and areas of improvement.

Conclusion:

The customer and marketing analytics transformation case study emphasizes the power of utilizing advanced Power Query techniques to drive actionable insights from customer and marketing data. By collecting, integrating, cleansing, validating, segmenting, analyzing, and visualizing customer and marketing data, businesses can better understand customer behaviors, optimize marketing efforts, and enhance customer experiences. This case study demonstrates the practical application of these techniques in real-world scenarios, highlighting their role in guiding effective marketing strategies and fostering stronger customer relationships.

CHAPTER XV
Future Trends in Data Transformation

15.1 Evolving Landscape of Data Transformation

As we look ahead to the future, the landscape of data transformation continues to evolve rapidly. In this chapter, we will explore the emerging trends, technologies, and practices that are shaping the way data is transformed and utilized. These trends have the potential to revolutionize data transformation processes, making them more efficient, flexible, and powerful. Let's delve into some of the key trends that are expected to shape the future of data transformation.

Trend 1: Automation and AI-Powered Transformation

Automation and artificial intelligence (AI) are poised to play a significant role in data transformation. AI-driven algorithms can analyze and interpret complex data structures, suggesting transformations and optimizations automatically. For instance, AI can identify patterns in data and recommend suitable data cleaning and transformation steps. Automated transformation workflows can streamline processes and reduce the manual effort required.

Trend 2: Cloud-Based Transformation

Cloud computing offers scalability and flexibility, making it an ideal platform for data transformation. Cloud-based data transformation tools allow teams to collaborate on data projects, access resources from anywhere, and scale up or down based on demand. Cloud-native transformations enable seamless integration with various data sources and advanced analytics platforms.

Trend 3: Real-Time and Streaming Transformations

As businesses increasingly rely on real-time data for decision-making, the need for real-time data transformation grows. Streaming data transformation platforms allow organizations to process and transform data as it arrives, enabling instantaneous insights and faster reactions to changing conditions. This is particularly valuable in industries such as finance, e-commerce, and IoT.

Trend 4: Self-Service Data Transformation

Empowering business users and domain experts to perform data transformations without deep technical expertise is a rising trend. Self-service data transformation tools provide intuitive interfaces and guided workflows, allowing non-technical users to clean, transform, and analyze data independently. This democratization of data transformation enhances agility and reduces bottlenecks.

Trend 5: Blockchain-Enabled Data Transformation

Blockchain technology's immutability and transparency offer a new dimension to data transformation. It can be used to create trusted audit trails for data transformation processes, ensuring data integrity and traceability. Blockchain-enabled transformations can enhance data governance and compliance, particularly in industries with stringent regulatory requirements.

Trend 6: Integration of Structured and Unstructured Data

The distinction between structured and unstructured data is blurring, with organizations recognizing the value of both types of data. Advanced data transformation techniques will focus on integrating and transforming structured and unstructured data seamlessly. Natural language processing and sentiment analysis can be integrated into transformation workflows for richer insights.

KIET HUYNH

Trend 7: Privacy-Preserving Transformations

As data privacy regulations become more stringent, privacy-preserving transformations are gaining importance. Techniques like differential privacy and homomorphic encryption allow organizations to transform and analyze data without exposing sensitive information. These methods strike a balance between data utility and privacy compliance.

Trend 8: Edge and Fog Computing Transformations

Edge and fog computing involve processing data closer to the source, reducing latency and enabling quicker decision-making. Data transformations performed at the edge can preprocess and filter data before sending it to centralized systems, optimizing bandwidth and reducing processing load on centralized servers.

Trend 9: Context-Aware Transformations

Context-aware transformations involve understanding the context in which data is generated or used. Contextual information can be leveraged to adapt data transformations dynamically, ensuring that data remains relevant and accurate within specific contexts.

Trend 10: Ethics and Bias Mitigation in Transformations

As data transformation plays a crucial role in data analysis and decision-making, addressing ethical concerns and biases becomes paramount. Future data transformation practices will prioritize the detection and mitigation of biases to ensure fair and equitable results.

Conclusion:

The evolving landscape of data transformation is marked by technological advancements and innovative approaches. As automation, cloud computing, real-time processing, and other trends continue to shape the field, data professionals need to stay current with these developments to unlock the full potential of their data. Embracing these trends will not only streamline data transformation processes but also pave the way for more informed decision-making and transformative business outcomes.

15.2 AI and Automation in Data Transformation

In the rapidly evolving landscape of data transformation, the integration of artificial intelligence (AI) and automation is becoming a game-changer. The synergy of AI and automation is revolutionizing how data is processed, cleaned, transformed, and analyzed. This chapter delves into the profound impact of AI and automation on data transformation and provides practical insights into implementing these trends effectively.

The Power of AI in Data Transformation:

AI technologies such as machine learning and deep learning are reshaping data transformation by automating complex tasks and driving data-driven insights. These technologies can be applied across various stages of data transformation:

1. Data Cleaning and Preprocessing: AI algorithms can automatically identify and rectify errors, inconsistencies, and missing values in the data. For example, AI can detect outliers and impute missing values using patterns learned from the existing data.

2. Pattern Recognition and Extraction: AI can identify intricate patterns in large datasets, enabling the extraction of meaningful features for further analysis. This is particularly useful in image recognition, natural language processing, and anomaly detection.

3. Transformation Rule Generation: AI can generate transformation rules based on historical data patterns. For instance, it can learn from past sales data to automatically predict and apply seasonal adjustments to future sales forecasts.

4. Automated Data Transformation Workflows: AI can analyze the structure and content of datasets to recommend suitable transformation steps. It can also optimize the order of transformations to minimize errors and improve processing efficiency.

Automation and Workflow Streamlining:

Automation streamlines data transformation processes by reducing manual intervention, minimizing errors, and increasing efficiency. Here's how to harness the power of automation in data transformation:

1. Workflow Orchestration: Use automation tools to create end-to-end data transformation workflows. These tools can schedule and trigger transformations based on specific conditions or time intervals.

2. Automated Data Ingestion: Set up automated data ingestion pipelines that pull data from various sources, transforming it as it's loaded. This ensures that data is always up-to-date and ready for analysis.

3. Rule-Based Transformations: Define transformation rules using if-then statements or decision trees. Automation tools can then apply these rules consistently to large datasets, ensuring standardized transformations.

4. Alerts and Notifications: Configure automated alerts and notifications to notify stakeholders when data quality issues or anomalies are detected during transformation processes.

Implementing AI and Automation: A Step-by-Step Guide:

1. Identify Transformation Needs: Assess your data transformation needs and challenges. Determine where AI and automation can provide the most value, such as data cleaning, feature extraction, or predictive modeling.

2. Data Preparation: Ensure your data is clean, structured, and well-prepared for AI and automation. This may involve data cleaning, normalization, and feature engineering.

3. Algorithm Selection: Choose suitable AI algorithms based on the nature of your data and the desired outcome. For example, use clustering algorithms for segmenting customers, or use regression algorithms for predicting numerical values.

4. Model Training: Train AI models using historical data. Use labeled data for supervised learning or unlabelled data for unsupervised learning. Continuously refine and fine-tune your models to improve accuracy.

5. Integration with Automation: Integrate your trained AI models into automated workflows. Set up triggers and conditions that initiate transformations based on specific events or data changes.

6. Testing and Validation: Thoroughly test your automated AI-driven transformations using validation datasets. Ensure that the transformations produce accurate results and meet your business objectives.

7. Continuous Monitoring and Improvement: Implement monitoring mechanisms to track the performance of your AI-driven transformations over time. Regularly evaluate the accuracy and efficiency of the transformations and make necessary adjustments.

Real-World Example: Customer Segmentation Using AI and Automation:

Imagine a retail company aiming to better understand its customer base for targeted marketing campaigns. Here's how AI and automation can help:

1. Data Collection: The company collects customer data from various sources, including purchase history, demographics, and online behavior.

2. Data Preparation: AI algorithms automatically clean and preprocess the data, handling missing values and outliers.

3. Feature Extraction: AI identifies relevant features such as spending patterns, frequency of purchases, and preferred product categories.

4. AI-Driven Transformation: Machine learning algorithms segment customers into distinct groups based on their purchasing behaviors. Automation triggers these transformations whenever new customer data is added.

5. Automated Marketing: The company uses these customer segments to create personalized marketing campaigns. Automation ensures that the right promotions reach the right customers at the right time.

Conclusion:

AI and automation are transforming data transformation from a labor-intensive process to a dynamic, intelligent, and efficient endeavor. By leveraging AI's analytical capabilities and automation's operational efficiency, organizations can unlock deeper insights from their data and make informed decisions faster than ever before. As AI algorithms continue to advance and automation tools become more sophisticated, data professionals will be well-equipped to navigate the data transformation landscape of the future.

15.3 Predictive Analytics and Beyond

As data continues to play an increasingly pivotal role in shaping business decisions, the integration of predictive analytics into data transformation processes holds immense potential. Predictive analytics involves the use of historical and current data to make predictions about future outcomes. This chapter explores the expanding role of predictive analytics in data transformation and how organizations can harness its capabilities to gain a competitive edge.

The Power of Predictive Analytics in Data Transformation:

Predictive analytics extends beyond traditional data transformation by enabling organizations to forecast trends, anticipate customer behaviors, optimize resource allocation, and enhance decision-making. It leverages machine learning algorithms and statistical models to make informed predictions about future events. This integration opens up new avenues for data transformation:

1. Enhanced Business Insights: Predictive analytics can uncover hidden patterns, relationships, and correlations within the data, enabling organizations to make proactive decisions and identify opportunities for growth.

2. Risk Assessment: Organizations can use predictive models to assess risks and potential outcomes. For example, financial institutions can predict credit default based on customer behavior and historical data.

3. Demand Forecasting: Predictive analytics assists in accurately forecasting demand for products and services, enabling efficient inventory management and production planning.

4. Customer Personalization: By analyzing past customer behavior, predictive analytics helps tailor personalized experiences, recommendations, and marketing campaigns.

5. Resource Optimization: Industries such as healthcare can use predictive analytics to optimize resource allocation, from bed availability in hospitals to distribution of medical supplies.

Implementing Predictive Analytics in Data Transformation:

1. Define Objectives: Clearly define the goals of your predictive analytics initiative. Identify the specific outcomes you aim to predict and the business problems you intend to solve.

2. Data Collection and Preparation: Gather historical data relevant to your prediction objectives. Cleanse and preprocess the data to ensure accuracy and consistency.

3. Feature Engineering: Identify relevant features that could impact the prediction. This step may involve transforming raw data into meaningful attributes for modeling.

4. Model Selection: Choose appropriate predictive modeling techniques based on your data and objectives. Common techniques include regression, classification, time series analysis, and machine learning algorithms.

5. Training and Validation: Split your data into training and validation sets. Train your predictive models on the training set and validate their performance using the validation set.

6. Model Evaluation: Assess the performance of your predictive models using evaluation metrics such as accuracy, precision, recall, and F1-score. Fine-tune the models to improve their performance.

7. Integration with Transformation Workflow: Integrate the predictive models into your data transformation workflow. Automate the process of applying predictive models to new data as it becomes available.

8. Monitoring and Maintenance: Continuously monitor the performance of your predictive models in real-world scenarios. Retrain models periodically to adapt to changing data patterns.

Real-World Example: Predictive Analytics for Customer Churn:

Consider a telecommunications company aiming to reduce customer churn (the rate at which customers leave their service). Here's how predictive analytics can help:

1. Data Collection: The company gathers historical customer data, including usage patterns, billing information, customer service interactions, and churn history.

2. Feature Selection: Relevant features include customer tenure, usage frequency, payment history, and customer interactions.

3. Predictive Model: The company chooses a classification algorithm, such as a random forest or logistic regression, to predict which customers are likely to churn.

4. Training and Validation: The model is trained on historical data with labeled churn outcomes. It's then validated using a holdout dataset to assess its accuracy.

5. Integration: The predictive model is integrated into the company's customer management system. As new customer data is collected, the model predicts churn likelihood.

6. Intervention Strategies: The company uses the predictions to identify high-risk customers and implement targeted retention strategies, such as offering discounts or personalized offers.

Predictive Analytics and Ethical Considerations:

While predictive analytics holds significant promise, it also raises ethical considerations related to privacy, bias, and fairness. It's crucial to ensure that predictive models are developed and applied responsibly, with proper safeguards in place to prevent discriminatory outcomes and protect sensitive information.

Conclusion:

Predictive analytics marks a pivotal advancement in data transformation, enabling organizations to move beyond historical insights and make predictions that shape future strategies. By integrating predictive analytics into data transformation workflows, organizations can make smarter decisions, enhance customer experiences, optimize operations, and remain agile in an ever-changing business landscape. However, this transformation comes with a responsibility to use predictive analytics ethically and transparently, ensuring that the insights generated benefit all stakeholders. As predictive analytics techniques continue to evolve, businesses that embrace these trends stand to gain a competitive advantage in the data-driven era.

Appendix
Power Query Formula Reference

A.1 Common Power Query Functions and Syntax

The Power Query formula language is a powerful tool for data transformation and manipulation. This appendix provides a reference guide to common Power Query functions and syntax, equipping you with the knowledge to efficiently transform your data. Below are some essential functions and their practical usage examples:

1. Data Loading:

- Table.FromRecords: Create a table from a list of records.

```PowerQuery
let
    data = [Name="John", Age=30, City="New York"],
    table = Table.FromRecords({data})
in
    table
```

- Csv.Document: Load data from a CSV file.

```PowerQuery
let
    source = Csv.Document(File.Contents("data.csv"), [Delimiter=",", Encoding=1252, QuoteStyle=QuoteStyle.Csv])
```

```
in

    source

```

2. Data Transformation:

- Table.TransformColumns: Apply a transformation to specific columns.

```PowerQuery
let

    source = Table.FromRecords({[Name="Alice", Age=25], [Name="Bob", Age=32]}),

    transformed = Table.TransformColumns(source, {{"Age", each _ * 2, Int64.Type}})

in

    transformed

```

- Table.AddColumn: Add a new column based on existing ones.

```PowerQuery
let

    source = Table.FromRecords({[Name="Carol", Age=28], [Name="David", Age=40]}),

    addedColumn = Table.AddColumn(source, "AgeGroup", each if [Age] < 30 then "Young" else "Adult")

in

    addedColumn

```

3. Filtering and Sorting:

- Table.SelectRows: Filter rows based on a condition.

```PowerQuery
let
    source = Table.FromRecords({[Name="Eve", Age=22], [Name="Frank", Age=50]}),
    filteredRows = Table.SelectRows(source, each [Age] > 25)
in
    filteredRows
```

- Table.Sort: Sort the table by one or more columns.

```PowerQuery
let
    source = Table.FromRecords({[Name="Grace", Age=35], [Name="Henry", Age=28]}),
    sortedTable = Table.Sort(source, {{"Age", Order.Ascending}})
in
    sortedTable
```

4. Aggregation:

- Table.Group: Group data and perform aggregate operations.

```PowerQuery
let
    source = Table.FromRecords({[City="London", Sales=100], [City="Paris", Sales=150], [City="London", Sales=200]}),
```

```
    groupedTable = Table.Group(source, {"City"}, {{"TotalSales", each List.Sum([Sales]),
type number}})

  in

    groupedTable

```
```

5. Merging and Joining:

- **Table.Join:** Join two tables based on common columns.

```PowerQuery

let

    table1 = Table.FromRecords({[ID=1, Name="Alice"], [ID=2, Name="Bob"]}),

    table2 = Table.FromRecords({[ID=1, Age=25], [ID=3, Age=30]}),

    joinedTable = Table.Join(table1, "ID", table2, "ID", JoinKind.LeftOuter)

in

    joinedTable

```
```

6. Custom Functions:

- **let...in:** Define and use custom functions within your queries.

```PowerQuery

let

    doubleValue = (x) => x * 2,

    source = Table.FromRecords({[Value=5], [Value=8]}),

    transformed = Table.AddColumn(source, "Doubled", each doubleValue([Value]))

in
```

transformed

```

```

Conclusion:

This Power Query formula reference provides a starting point for mastering the art of data transformation. By utilizing these common functions and syntax, you can efficiently shape your data to suit your analytical needs. As you become more comfortable with the language, you'll discover the flexibility and power it offers in handling even the most complex data transformation challenges. Experiment with these functions and explore additional ones to become a proficient Power Query user.

A.2 Advanced Power Query Techniques and Combinations

In this section, we will delve into advanced Power Query techniques and combinations that allow you to tackle intricate data transformation challenges. These techniques involve leveraging multiple functions and strategies in combination to achieve complex transformations. Let's explore some practical examples:

1. Dynamic Column Creation:

Example 1: Calculating Growth Rate

You can dynamically create columns to calculate growth rates for different periods.

```PowerQuery
let

    source = Table.FromRecords({[Year=2019, Sales=1000], [Year=2020, Sales=1200], [Year=2021, Sales=1500]}),

    years = source[Year],
```

```
calculateGrowth = (year) => (source[Sales]{List.PositionOf(years, year)} -
source[Sales]{List.PositionOf(years, year) - 1}) / source[Sales]{List.PositionOf(years, year) -
1},

    transformed = Table.FromColumns(Table.ToColumns(source) & List.Transform(years, each
{Text.From(_) & " Growth", calculateGrowth(_)}))

in

    transformed
```

2. Hierarchical Aggregations and Combining Data:

Example 1: Combining Sales Data with Hierarchical Categories

You can combine sales data from multiple sources and create custom hierarchical aggregations.

```PowerQuery
let

    salesData = Table.FromRecords({[Category="Electronics", Product="TV", Sales=1000],
[Category="Electronics", Product="Laptop", Sales=1500], [Category="Clothing",
Product="Shirt", Sales=500]}),

    categoryAggregates = Table.Group(salesData, {"Category"}, {{"TotalSales", each
List.Sum([Sales]), type number}}),

    combined = Table.NestedJoin(salesData, {"Category"}, categoryAggregates, {"Category"},
"CategoryAggregates"),

    expanded = Table.ExpandTableColumn(combined, "CategoryAggregates", {"TotalSales"})

in

    expanded
```

3. Advanced Date and Time Transformations:

Example 1: Calculating Moving Averages

Calculate moving averages for a time series using a custom function.

```PowerQuery
let

    timeSeries = Table.FromRecords({[Date=#date(2020, 1, 1), Value=10], [Date=#date(2020, 1, 2), Value=15], [Date=#date(2020, 1, 3), Value=20]}),

    movingAverage = (values, window) => List.Average(List.FirstN(values, window)),

    windowSize = 2,

    transformed = Table.AddColumn(timeSeries, "MovingAverage", each movingAverage(Table.Column(timeSeries, "Value"), windowSize))

in

    transformed
```

4. Custom Function Iteration:

Example 1: Applying Custom Function to List Elements

Apply a custom function to elements of a list using `List.Transform`.

```PowerQuery
let

    numbers = {1, 2, 3, 4, 5},

    square = (x) => x * x,

    squaredNumbers = List.Transform(numbers, each square(_))
```

in

squaredNumbers

```
```

5. Pivot and Unpivot Techniques:

Example 1: Unpivoting Multiple Columns into Key-Value Pairs

Unpivot multiple columns into key-value pairs using `Table.UnpivotOtherColumns`.

```PowerQuery
let
    source = Table.FromRecords({[ID=1, JanSales=100, FebSales=150], [ID=2, JanSales=200, FebSales=180]}),
    unpivoted = Table.UnpivotOtherColumns(source, {"ID"}, "Month", "Sales")
in
    unpivoted
```

Conclusion:

In this appendix, we've explored advanced Power Query techniques and their combinations that can be employed to address complex data transformation scenarios. By creatively combining functions and strategies, you can unlock the full potential of Power Query and efficiently manipulate data to meet your specific needs. These examples provide you with a foundation to experiment with various techniques and develop your solutions for intricate data challenges. As you become more adept at combining these techniques, you'll be well-equipped to tackle even the most intricate data transformation tasks with confidence and efficiency.

Conclusion

Congratulations! You've reached the end of "Advanced Power Query Techniques: Transforming and Shaping Data Like a Pro." Throughout this book, we've embarked on a journey to explore the depths of Power Query and unlock its full potential for data transformation. From handling complex data structures to leveraging advanced text manipulation, conditional logic, and aggregation techniques, you've gained a comprehensive understanding of how to wield Power Query as a powerful tool in your data toolkit.

By delving into real-world case studies and practical examples, you've not only learned the theory behind advanced techniques but also witnessed their application in various contexts. The combination of detailed explanations, concrete examples, and step-by-step instructions has provided you with the knowledge and skills necessary to tackle intricate data challenges with confidence.

As you continue your journey in the realm of data transformation, remember that mastery comes through practice. Experiment with the techniques you've learned, adapt them to your specific projects, and explore the endless possibilities that Power Query offers. The landscape of data transformation is ever-evolving, and your newfound expertise will serve as a solid foundation to navigate these changes.

Thank You for Your Support

We want to express our sincere gratitude for choosing "Advanced Power Query Techniques: Transforming and Shaping Data Like a Pro." Your commitment to expanding your skills and knowledge in the world of data transformation is commendable. We hope this book has provided you with valuable insights and practical tools that will empower you to excel in your data-driven endeavors.

If you have any feedback, questions, or further inquiries, please don't hesitate to reach out to us. Your input is invaluable in helping us enhance our content and support your ongoing learning journey.

Once again, thank you for being a part of this journey. We wish you all the success in mastering advanced Power Query techniques and achieving your data transformation goals.

Printed in Great Britain
by Amazon